Methuen Playscripts

The Methuen Playscripts series exists to extend the range of plays in print by publishing work which is not yet widely known but which has already earned a place in the acting repertoire of the modern theatre.

The Pleasure Principle

Snoo Wilson's new full-length play was first staged at the Royal Court Theatre Upstairs in November 1973.

'At the bottom of it all we want to have the best time of all, and in practical terms we always settle for less. We always frustrate those sudden urges. Tonight, the middle way, a little pleasure. Not too much of anything, because in this world you lose it all that way, you end up unhappy or dead. That's *our* pleasure principle. No extravagant responses, please . . . ' Despite the moderate tone of this counsel to the audience, the play itself excels in sharp dialogue, brilliant inventiveness, and ironic reversals, varying on themes of sex, wealth and violence, which, in the words of one reviewer, proclaim that moderation is the eighth deadly sin.

'Unquestionably, *The Pleasure Principle* is the most heartening new play to have emerged this year from the old power-house in Sloane Square.'
Frank Marcus in *The Sunday Telegraph*

' . . . suggests an unholy miscegenation between the Crazy Gang and Jean-Luc Godard. On the one hand it is a strenuous indictment of ownership, property, greed and personal exploitation: on the other, it is a madhouse extravaganza that operates on the good old comic principle of always putting a bomb under the audience's expectations.'
Michael Billington in *The Guardian*

THE
PLEASURE
PRINCIPLE

**The Politics of Love,
the Capital of Emotion**

SNOO WILSON

First published in Great Britain 1974
by Eyre Methuen Ltd
11 New Fetter Lane, London EC4P 4EE
Copyright © 1974 Snoo Wilson

Set by Expression Typesetters
Printed in Great Britain by
Fletcher & Son Ltd, Norwich

ISBN 0 413 32000 6 (cased)
ISBN 0 413 32010 3 (paperback)

CAUTION

For David Hare, the Cast and the Stage Management
of the Theatre Upstairs

The Pleasure Principle was first performed at the Royal Court Theatre Upstairs on 26 November 1973 with the following cast:

GALE	Julie Covington
MARIEN	Ann Firbank
ROBERT	Dinsdale Landen
MACK	Stewart Harwood
JOAN	Brenda Fricker
ALKO McCOY	Bob Sherman
AEROPLANE PARKER and GORILLA	George Fenton
ZOBNEZ KERSABIEC and GORILLA	Neil Fitzwilliam

Directed by David Hare
Designed by Harriet Geddes
Lighting by Nick Heppel
Sound by Ras Compton

ACT ONE

Blackout: countdown and first two bars of Sha-Na-Na, 'At the Hop'. Then cut sound, lights up.

Two carpets, one upstage left and one downstage right, both about six foot square.

On the upstage carpet area there are twin hotel beds, with nauseous pink candlewick bedspreads, and enough hotel furniture to establish it as such, with a litter of suitcases in the foreground, chaotically around GALE's bed, obsessive neatness around MARIEN's.

On the downstage area, yet to be lit, there is a Wimpy Bar table and two stools.

GALE and MARIEN are sitting amidst the luggage. They are a day or so into a holiday in western Ireland and are already bored. The conversation has that mixture of tetchiness and artificial brightness common to those who have known each other for some time and are determined to have a good time in spite of it.

GALE is lying down, partially relaxed, MARIEN is on the edge of her bed rather more tense. GALE is reading a copy of *Woman*. Slowly without looking she pushes one shoe off. It drops to the floor.

A long pause. Suddenly MARIEN reaches across and takes the other one off.

GALE: What are you doing?

MARIEN: I couldn't bear the strain of waiting!

(Pause.)

What happens then?

GALE (flipping through *Woman*): Oh, they come back together and gaze warmly into each other's eyes over what must be an Access Card dinner if he's only just got his job back. Did you know, they ban this if it has contraceptive advice in it? Joan told me —

MARIEN: And then?

GALE: There's an article on should you let your daughter, and the answer is yes, but not with that dubious Italian waiter she's been seeing so much of, with his soiled jacket, dirty fingernails and nasty greasy lips. Do you think the readers of this enjoy making love?

MARIEN: You told me you didn't.

GALE: It's true. I don't. Haven't for years.

MARIEN: Really — ?

GALE: Something always gets in the way, and the fishy smell always puts me off —

MARIEN: You know, when I'm with you, I sometimes feel a bit like the BBC. I can stand politics, I can take any amount of undressing, but *nastiness* — yeoghugh!

(Pause.)

I'm sure that taxi overcharged us.

GALE: Yes . . .

MARIEN (at a loose end): Gale, your knickers are under the bed — did you know that?

GALE: Yes.

MARIEN: There are chests of drawers here you know — it's not like your flat.

(Pause.)

GALE: A question dear coz.

(Pause.)

Why did we come to Ireland?

MARIEN: Oh — Gale —

GALE: D'you think we're punishing ourselves?

MARIEN: We looked at a map and —

GALE: It all looked the same. From the train.

MARIEN (an attempted lecture): Plainly, the large river is the Shannon —

GALE: Why didn't the train climb these hills?

MARIEN: We're at the edge!

GALE: The edge of the soup plate.

MARIEN: The hills keep the water out, not in.

GALE: A dried-out soup plate.

MARIEN: It was rather bleak.

GALE: Brown Windsor.

MARIEN: Topographically, we aren't probably very sophisticated.

(Pause. Then, brightly.)

We'll have to go and meet *people* instead.

(Pause.)

GALE: Do you know, Byron went to Corsica, and found all the bandits wearing stays?

MARIEN: How disappointing for him.

GALE: Who would have thought that bandits would dress up like that? It must have been the effect of the beauty all around them.

MARIEN: You mean they didn't have the excuse of living in a rural slum
 like here.

 (Justification.)

 You know, people find this beautiful.

GALE: I'm not *criticising* our holiday.

MARIEN: You just can't stand the hills and the rain.

 (Pause.)

 Further on, you know, there's the sea.

GALE: I suppose there will always be slums in nature, there will always be
 slums in the cities —

MARIEN: It just so happens the poor Irish have both.

GALE: We're being ridiculous. Of course it's not the Mediterranean, but
 it's got to have merits apart from what we can see, because people have
 loved it and died for it.

MARIEN: It is dull.

GALE: No —

MARIEN: My mind's made up.

GALE: I do envy you sometimes, Marien. You're just bursting with decisions
 . . . It's the sort of person you are. When I had anorexia, you know,
 couldn't eat — I asked Jameson, why me, and he said, that's the sort of
 person you are. I told him I'd stopped making love — he wanted to examine
 me. I said, there's nothing wrong with my *body*. It's my mind, I just
 cannot decide whether or not . . .

 (Pause.)

MARIEN: Let's go and eat.

GALE: Oh, I don't know —

MARIEN: At least it's something to do —

GALE: Can I think about it?

MARIEN: Really, you're still as dithery as ever! One has to treat you like a
 child to get things done —

GALE: Let's eat at the hotel.

MARIEN: It's after eight. There's only the Wimpy open.

GALE: Suppose they don't have the food I want?

MARIEN: Well?

GALE (triumph of logic): Then I'll have gone out for nothing!

MARIEN (muttered angrily): Exactly the same as when you were small.

 (Out loud.)

We're on *holiday,* Gale. It's the only place open and —

GALE: I'm thinking.

MARIEN: You don't have to *think*!

GALE: I'll stay here and read.

(Sudden decision.)

I don't want to go out.

(Tableau. MARIEN disquieted.

GALE starts to read *Woman* sitting on the bed.

Suddenly after a pause, MARIEN gets up and gets a scarf and goes up silently behind GALE and calmly blindfolds her from behind.

GALE stays quite still.)

GALE (morosely): Why all this appeal to childhood loyalties, childhood games? I hated staying with you in the holidays, if you must know. You were too old for me.

MARIEN (bright): I know, you always have to be jollied along —

GALE (a terrible insistence): You were too old for me.

MARIEN (flat, finishing the knot): That's what Robert says.

GALE: About him or me?

MARIEN: Him.

(Pause.)

There's no redress against that.

(They are still in the same position on the bed, MARIEN having tied the knot in the blindfold.

Pause.)

GALE: Here we go.

(Gets up.)

We're on the way from hysterical misery to plain ordinary human unhappiness.

(Blackout area. Sound cue: 'Performance' first few bars. The actresses laugh. The lights come up on the Wimpy Bar area and MARIEN and GALE walk into the light. MARIEN guides GALE with great solicitude and they sit down close to each other. She is still blindfolded.)

MARIEN (to GALE): All right?

GALE: You'd hardly know we were moving.

(Pause.)

I imagine we are a spectacle.

(Pause.)

Read me the menu.

MARIEN: Bender the meaty frankfurter. Egg Brunch, Shanty Brunch, Delta the succulent porkburger.

GALE (flatly): Unimaginable.

MARIEN: There are pictures.

GALE: My mind's a blank.

MARIEN: An International is a Wimpy Bender, Delta and French friend potatoes.

(Pause.)

Shall I go on?

GALE: One is tempted to emulate Proust's florid indecision when deciding whether to stay for another chorus of *Rigoletto*.

MARIEN (sharp): Don't.

GALE (undeterred): Madeleineburgers?

(Pause.)

MARIEN (ploughing on): Brown Derby, Knickerbocker Glory or Chocolate Bonanza.

GALE: Could I have a glass of water d'you think?

MARIEN: There's no waiter yet.

GALE (suddenly brusque): Invent one.

MARIEN: I'm terrible at waiters.

GALE: Yes.

MARIEN: This is such hard work.

GALE: It's fun.

(Pause.)

MARIEN (suddenly): Robert wants to come and stay with us.

GALE: No.

MARIEN: It would only be friendly. They say he's very lonely.

GALE (crushing): Who are '*they*'?

MARIEN: I think it's partly nostalgia — the divorce isn't recognised in Ireland — we were married in Dublin.

GALE: How sick-making.

MARIEN: What's wrong?

GALE: I'd feel uncomfortable. We arranged to have a complete spinster's holiday —

MARIEN (pleading): You can't just *leave* people when they're in trouble. And anyhow, he's on holiday too.

GALE: Isn't he spending all his money or something?

MARIEN: He buys and sells houses as he moves around.

GALE: That won't keep him forever.

MARIEN: It would, if only he'd buy the right ones. He's still got most of the £150,000 he was given.

GALE: I suppose he'll go around snapping up Galway turf cottages and letting them to sensitive painters. That sort of exploitation really sickens me.

MARIEN (definitively): All right then, not.

(Pause. A cautious introductory note.)

He's planning to bring a car. He wants to drive down to round Cork and have a look at property there.

GALE: Dull.

MARIEN: More interesting than Westport . . .

GALE (emphatic): I have nothing to say to him: he's mad . . .

MARIEN: Anyone over forty goes mad . . . .

GALE: When he tried to seduce me he told me such *lies* . . .

(Pause.)

He'll try to screw one of us.

MARIEN: He's got a chauffeur.

GALE: Why does he need a chauffeur? He can drive!

MARIEN: He was breathalysed, but he had joined this wonderful scheme which helps one with the cost of a chauffeur if one's stopped from driving oneself.

GALE: Why can't he catch the train?

MARIEN: He *adores* the car.

GALE (biting): What a fool.

(Pause.)

You know, we're not going to get served here, we're too odd.

(Pause. GALE's hands move over the table. She drums fingers. Then she finds a piece of paper. Holds it.)

GALE: What's this? A dirty postcard?

MARIEN (without looking): A bill.

GALE: I want exactly what they had.

MARIEN (taking the piece of paper): There might be more than one . . .

GALE: I'll make a pig of myself.

MARIEN: It says –

GALE: I'm burning with anticipation.

MARIEN: It's so difficult − I left my reading spectacles in our room.

GALE: Come on!

MARIEN (as if reading a crossword clue): It says − there's a bomb in here, you've got ten minutes to get out.

(Blackout.

Instantly, a followspot picks out ROBERT and MACK, dancing, downstage left, dressed as they will first appear.

ROBERT wearing a white or very light grey double-breasted suit, MACK in an archaic cut of chauffeur's uniform, with boots and the trousers cut like jodhpurs.

Sound cue, Edith Piaf singing, "Non, Je Ne Regrette Rien".

ROBERT and MACK waltz luxuriously to this tune.

GALE and MARIEN go back to the hotel.

When they have got out of the way, MACK and ROBERT waltz across the stage together and disappear, whereupon their spot is cut, and the music fades away quickly.

The hotel lights come up immediately, and we see GALE lying and MARIEN sitting on their respective beds, which are now unmade.

As before, the tension emanates from MARIEN, and GALE lets her do the worrying.

GALE is reading *Woman.*

Pause. MARIEN is staring hard at GALE.)

GALE (without looking up): I want to go for a walk.

(Pause.)

MARIEN: It's raining.

(Pause.)

GALE (still not looking up): Nothing new. I'll go by myself.

MARIEN: I'd feel happier if neither of us went out alone.

GALE (off-hand): Are you still shaky?

MARIEN (incredulous): Did you think I was *joking*?

GALE: I was just going along with it. When it did go off, I thought, that's very small, for a bomb, but she's not joking.

(Turns the page.)

Still, we were some distance up the road.

MARIEN: We'd hardly left −

GALE: I counted two hundred paces.

MARIEN: The skin of our teeth —

GALE: That butcher across the street who was putting up the shutters only got sprayed with glass.

MARIEN (incredulous): We were inside. We would have beeen killed!

GALE (offhand): Thanks for saving my life, anyhow.

(Pause.)

I do wish you hadn't rung Robert though.

MARIEN: I was afraid!

(JOAN, the hotel maid, comes in.)

Joan.

JOAN: I heard you had a terrible time last night. And did you escape by the skin of your teeth? —

MARIEN (crisply): Yes —

JOAN: And which one was the hostage?

MARIEN: The — ?

JOAN: The blindfold hostage.

GALE: Oh that was me. But we were just playing a game, Marien and I.

JOAN: Will you ever tell us what it was that happened?

MARIEN (grimly): We're just trying to decide ourselves.

JOAN: But you're not hurt.

MARIEN: Well we won't know until we find out, will we?

GALE (crushed): We're perfectly all right thank you, Joan. We're leaving today.

JOAN: It won't happen again you know; there's a fierce crowd of Garda round the town.

MARIEN: Someone's coming to collect us.

JOAN: Will I take the sheets off?

(GALE makes no attempt to get out of bed so MARIEN stands and JOAN takes the sheets off her bed.)

MARIEN: Gale, you could be packing now.

GALE: Joan, what do you think of it all?

JOAN: We've never had any trouble here before, except from some long-haired hippies out in the bay, it's the fishing mostly. Hardly anyone went to the Wimpy Bar when they were here because they were either drinking or they went to bed after fishing all day.

GALE: Who did it?

JOAN: It was the young men from Sligo put it there. They had a blue

Cortina.

MARIEN: Did anyone catch them?

JOAN: Oh no, they went back to Sligo.

(Pause.)

You're not leaving because of the explosion are you?

MARIEN (buttoned up): No, we had talked about it yesterday.

JOAN: It was only a little bomb.

MARIEN (even more buttoned): We noticed.

(Pause.)

No, someone's driving us down to Cork.

JOAN (ambassadorial): Oh, it is lovely country down there.

GALE: Are any of your family in England, Joan?

(JOAN has finished the one bed and folded the blankets. MARIEN pulls GALE out of the other bed. GALE sits down on MARIEN's stripped bed and JOAN gets to work on GALE's bed.)

JOAN: Don't bother yourselves — I can do it when you're gone — there's no one else coming.

MARIEN (grimly): No trouble.

JOAN (to GALE): I've five brothers there and if there's any justice in Heaven I'll be in London come the winter earning a decent wage. My dad drives a taxi sometimes but all the business was with the French and German fishers and they haven't come for two years. You'd think the whole town had died away sometimes . . . Tourists've got no idea of geography. There's generally no trouble here. It's all in the North.

GALE: You're a large family?

JOAN: Twelve, yes, and I'll put a bit by when I get something to send them.

MARIEN (businesslike): Perhaps Robert would give Joan a job.

GALE: Perhaps he wouldn't.

JOAN (to MARIEN): Is Robert your husband?

MARIEN: He was. Joan, how do *you* feel about coming back to London with us?

(JOAN immediately exits as GALE and MARIEN stare at each other. Pause.)

MARIEN: I haven't upset her have I?

GALE: It's a terrible fate to wish on anyone.

MARIEN: He's not that bad. Anyhow, she doesn't have to work for Robert: she could get a job somewhere else.

GALE: She's got a job here. Why mess her up?

MARIEN (throwaway): She didn't take it seriously —

(Patronising laugh.)

It doesn't say much for their national consciousness if they're prepared to leave at the drop of a hat.

GALE: Anyone can see she's dying to leave. This is all wrong: we shouldn't play with people who are in her position.

(Pause.)

MARIEN: She hardly knows us.

GALE (worried): She's probably very poorly paid here —

MARIEN: We haven't made any promises, have we. If she does come back we can just say no.

GALE (miserably): She'll be utterly humiliated.

MARIEN (annoyed at GALE): All right! We'll take her!

GALE: That's not what I mean. I mean I regret, intensely, that we ever placed ourselves in a position of frivolously offering employment, because we will disappoint her, and we have all the cards, and there is no redress against that disappointment.

MARIEN: She will be disappointed, certainly, if she doesn't come.

(Pause.)

We're giving her the opportunity to better herself.

GALE (contempt): Better!

MARIEN: If you came from a family of twelve, you'd do just about anything to speed up the cash flow. What future has she got here but to emigrate like everybody else? You're afraid of servants because you don't like the responsibility of looking after people.

GALE (angry): Of course you're right!

(Pause. Then icy.)

And you want to give Robert a little Irish girl as a present.

(Moral.)

People aren't *things*, you know.

MARIEN: She'd give her right arm to get out of this bog.

GALE (renewed attacked): It is civilised here you know. It's just a bit slower, that's all. People don't always have to be *doing* all the time.

MARIEN: What does she want?

(Rhetorical.)

She wants a bit more money, and a bit more action. She's young. All right, we won't take her, but in eighteen months she'll go anyway.

(Pause. Then magnificent.)

The life here plainly means nothing to her at all.

(Ironic.)

But because you can't stand the idea of responsibility, we'll say no.

(JOAN re-enters, this time changed, carrying a tiny white suitcase. She has a smart new coat on, and an inappropriate hat.

She sweeps in, picks up armfuls of GALE's unpacked luggage, MARIEN's packed luggage, while GALE and MARIEN simply look at her.)

JOAN (very quickly, and with great excitement): Sam, that's the porter here, tells me there's a big soft car outside with a man in it and a chauffeur up the front and if we can only go by way of the house to say goodbye to tell them I'm going, I've given my notice here and I'm ready.

(Blackout. Spot on a barrel at the side of the stage. Edith Piaf, a small waif-like person in black appears head and shoulders out of it, and sings solo 'Je Ne Regrette Rien'. The hotel and Wimpy are struck. Blackout spot.

The sound becomes birdsong, distant and intermittent, and the soft hiss of rain.

The light is soft, grey, suggestive of wet Ireland.

MACK, dressed in his chauffeur's uniform, runs on from stage left, carrying a packed-up family tent of vivid fluorescent orange. The tent is six foot square, and has an awning under which the lunch party may take place.

He erects it midstage left, facing towards the audience, at a slight angle to the rest of the stage. It has a small Union Jack on the top.

Business.

After a suitable length of time, GALE and MARIEN come on from the same side. They are both holding umbrellas, though not over their heads for most of the time.

Plainly it is the lightest of drizzles.

GALE and MARIEN are sharing a joke as they come on. GALE produces the punch line mid-stage.)

GALE: *He* said – "I work for Cunard" and *he* said – "Well I work fukken 'ard an' all, but I ain't got one of *them*!"

(They both laugh, naturally and briefly.

They stop midstage, turn, and watch MACK putting up the tent.

MARIEN puts her umbrella up. Plainly MARIEN and GALE's moods have been greatly improved.)

GALE (sotto voce, abstracted): It's so fresh . . .

(Pause.)

MARIEN: Isn't it just.

(Pause.)

GALE: I thought we were parking the tent by the river, to go swimming.

MARIEN: Mack — why are you setting up here?

MACK (carrying on): It's very boggy towards the foreshore.

MARIEN: Oh, how depressing.

MACK (stolid): It is, if you fall in.

(Pause.)

There's a path down there, a sheep run, might lead you to it.

(Pause.)

GALE (not looking): We really are far away.

MARIEN: Yes . . .

(Neither of them has the strength to tell MACK they want to move. The irritation starts to peter out.)

GALE: I didn't know it was so difficult.

(Querulous.)

I spent half an hour changing behind the only bush for *miles.*

(MARIEN lifts up GALE's coat from behind to look underneath.)

MARIEN (provocative): Good heavens.

GALE (moving away, embarrassed): Look leave me be.

MARIEN (sparkling with mischief): Let's have a look — is it a two-piece?

(GALE moves away from her again.)

I must say I thought you were having a piddle.

(GALE becomes extremely embarrassed. MARIEN moves in again.)

GALE: In the name of charity — Marien — for pity's sake let me be.

MARIEN (still intent): It's a blue one, we know that much.

MACK (who has not realised the source of confusion): If you want to swim, there's a sheep track will lead you to it in no time.

(Goes on with work.)

MARIEN (a sudden idea): Come on let's go down to the river.

GALE: You're not changed.

MARIEN: I'll just watch.

GALE: The trouble is, I know it'll be cold, and I won't be able to dry out properly when I get out.

MARIEN: My dear girl, the *sun*'ll be out in a minute —

(ROBERT enters from the same side as everyone else. He is dressed in the suit he wore earlier, and a close-weave panama hat with a florid riband round it.

Over his arm he carries a towel, a dressing-gown, a pair of bathing drawers, and a folded umbrella.)

ROBERT: No it won't.

(He goes inside the tent and disappears. MACK is putting the finishing touches to the tent.)

ROBERT (within): This isn't going to fall down is it, Mack?

MACK: It's safe now, it's all right.

(MACK stands up and surveys his work.)

ROBERT (within): Safe as houses.

(Pause.)

Mack, go and get the rest of the things will you?

MACK: Right.

(MACK goes off.

Pause. Then MARIEN calls out.)

MARIEN: Right!

(Pause.)

What are we having for lunch?

(Pause. Uncertainty.)

There will be enough — enough for all of us, as well as Joan?

ROBERT (within): Galantine of duck. Chicken in white sauce.

(Pause.)

Tiny tiny mushrooms.

(MARIEN goes over to where GALE is standing and whispers to her.)

MARIEN: You've got to ask him about Joan — now.

(GALE looks at her dismally.)

We agreed.

(GALE slowly turns round and goes to the mouth of the tent, now closed with ROBERT inside. She stands six feet away, composing herself to speak

Suddenly, ROBERT emerges. He is wearing a blue striped bathing tunic, sleeveless, coming down to mid-thigh.

Also he is wearing a crude plastic 'Professor' mask over the top of his face. Big plastic dome going half way back over his head, plastic nose, spectacles, cheeks and eyebrows all stuck together.

He poses arms akimbo.

GALE: I thought it was someone else.

ROBERT (keeping the arms akimbo): H. W. Fowler, author of *Modern English Usage*, or his brother, bathing in the sea off the Isle of Wight, 1905, a rare photograph.

(Brief tableau.

Slowly takes off the mask and throws it away.)

Halcyon days.

(JOAN and MACK come in carrying aluminium folding chairs which they set out by the tent, and a folding table which also is set out.)

ROBERT (approval): Good. Good. Wonderful people. Where's my umbrella Mack darling?

MACK: I was carrying the chairs.

ROBERT: Fair 'nuff. Don't forget it when you bring the hamper.

(ROBERT kisses MACK sweetly on the cheek.

He sits down having put up a chair for himself in front of the tent under the awning.

JOAN and MACK exit.

GALE and MARIEN are still standing uncertainly on the perimeter of all this activity.

ROBERT sits down and starts to cut his toenails.

The lights come up to a sunlight brightness.)

ROBERT (pleasure): Ah!

(GALE and MARIEN shift minutely, put their umbrellas away.

Pause. ROBERT clips away.)

ROBERT: I'll have to do this or it'll be bitter agony walking to the river.

MARIEN (invading the ceremony): Joan —

ROBERT (without looking up): She's gone to get the hamper.

MARIEN (irritated): Oh, Robert! Listen to me —

ROBERT: Can we have complete silence — this is extremely delicate —

MARIEN: I want to talk to you about Joan!

ROBERT: I can't possibly afford her.

(Pause.)

. . . The Christian Barnard of toejam . . .

MARIEN: I don't see why you have to draw the line at Joan.

ROBERT: Everything in moderation.

MARIEN: I do wish you wouldn't do that outside.

ROBERT (talking to his toe): Talk all day, never get off their arses except to drink

(Gombeen accent.)

Little pots of creamy top.

(Back to English.)

Guinness to you.

MARIEN: You are going to take her on.

ROBERT: I can't afford to be *more* extravagant.

MARIEN: For six weeks until she gets another job.

ROBERT: I knew somebody who had a grandmother, and someone came for lunch, and stayed for twenty-five years. And when she threw him out, she was sued.

MARIEN: Robert, this is important, I'm asking you as a favour —

ROBERT: Not bloody likely.

MARIEN: Don't *argue* Robert.

GALE: Argue about money or argue about your marriage but for God's sake do it in separate compartments.

ROBERT: Very good. We will separate out. I have lots of money, but no emotion. I will not pay people to leave home. It is not my responsibility.

GALE: But finally it *is* an emotional matter because she is under the illusion that you will because we foolishly allowed her to think so. So we have placed you rather tactlessly under an obligation. For which we apologise.

ROBERT: With me, money wins over love every time.

GALE: You know that's a heartless remark, and you know it isn't true. We're asking you because you can afford it.

ROBERT: What sort of fool d'you take me for? It won't make her any happier, and it's a terrible wrench for me. All those stories about mean rich people, they're true.

(Pause. Considered note.)

They're generally written from quite the wrong point of view.

(Pause. ROBERT starts to open a champagne bottle.)

People feel guilt about money. The only thing worth worrying about, if they want to feel guilty, is poverty, because it makes you impossible to live with. If you were poor, Gale, your personality wouldn't rip the skin off a rice pudding. So hang on to your money like grim death is my advice.

GALE (sudden collapse): All right, I'll pay for everything.

ROBERT: That's another mistake. Joan was probably very happy, leading a normal servant life. She'd never be that happy in London, she'll find the cost of living's doubled with her wage, it takes her ten times as long to get to work. She'll be very *un*happy. And we're arguing about her transport fee.

GALE: Please drop the subject.

ROBERT: I can talk for the rest of my life on how wrong it is to give money away.

I like my possessions. I have a dynamic relationship with them because they express me. My chauffeur expresses something about me. But I have nothing, nothing to do with Joan at all. We don't owe it to the Irish to employ them.

(MACK and JOAN reappear with the hamper and Robert's umbrella. They appear to be rather flustered.

ROBERT looks at them. He ruffles MACK's hair.)

When Marx was my age, or a bit younger perhaps, he was very worried because as a Jewish intellectual he felt he didn't know any members of the working class. Socially.

MARIEN: Joan, you look very red.

ROBERT: Mack's been getting up her in the back of the car. Unfaithful servant.

(He starts to ease the champagne cork out, pointing it at Joan's behind.)

MARIEN: Robert —

ROBERT: The spectre of international capitalism — me . . . stalking the rabbit of non-union labour and —

(He fires the cork. It hits JOAN.)

— Gotcha!

(JOAN pretends nothing has happened.)

Pause.

MACK starts laying the table.)

Knife on the right, Mack, in all cases.

JOAN: Will I help him?

ROBERT (indifferent): No. He's all right when he gets going.

ROBERT: Tell us about the bomb. It must have been frightful.

(The situation relaxes somewhat.)

MARIEN: Well Gale and I went to the Wimpy. I had blindfolded Gale —

ROBERT: You had — ?

MARIEN: Blindfolded Gale — she swore she couldn't see —

ROBERT (mock urbane): To go to a restaurant . . .

MARIEN (ignores this): Anyhow — there was this note — in a green felt-tipped pen, but tiny writing, which Gale found —

ROBERT: But she was blindfold.

MARIEN: She felt it. And the note said, you've got ten minutes to get out, there's a bomb in here.

ROBERT: You should have kept it. Souvenir.

MARIEN: And we ran up the road, with Gale still in the blindfold because I thought if she took it off she'd panic or, if I took it off . . .

ROBERT: Then?

MARIEN: And then the bomb went off.

ROBERT: And Gale still had her blindfold on.

MARIEN: Yes.

ROBERT: And then she took it off.

(Crushing.)

You two are quite extraordinary. Tell me why did they blow up the Wimpy.

MARIEN (lightly): Perhaps it was the only place open when they arrived.

GALE: It's not an Irish company.

MARIEN: It was the last thing you'd expect to find there.

JOAN: They were hoping to get the tourists.

MARIEN: That's what I said, why they built it.

JOAN: No, why they blew it up.

(Pause.)

MARIEN: I hope they're not coming round to finish the job.

JOAN: It's nothing personal.

ROBERT: What a deplorable state of affairs. Still, Ireland is like that because they can't control their destinies and if we're not careful England will go the same way. A quarter of British industry will be owned by America in 1980. The Irish can hate us, we should hate the Americans.

MACK (cheerful): I hate the Irish.

ROBERT: Ireland isn't a country really, it's a disease. You could wipe out the whole island, and it would still drag out its existence in the hearts of the exiles and their children, and their children's children . . .

JOAN: They say you could rebuild Dublin from James Joyce's books.

(Pause. Nobody takes this one up.)

ROBERT: My niece, who is five, said to me — admittedly a remark she parroted, Uncle, why are there so many Micks in London, and I said, for which I am doubtless already burning in hell, because of their benighted religion, they are obliged to fuck more carelessly.

JOAN (annoyed): Isn't five a little young for that sort of crude speaking?

ROBERT: The child's questions should be answered simply and naturally, or you create a mystery. The basis of a religion. The building blocks of repression. The history of Ireland.

(Pause.)

Let's eat.

(As the company rises to sit round the table.)

JOAN (upset): Five hundred years ago, we were all united in Christ.

ROBERT: Why is it that all sensitive and intelligent people end up having a conversation about another, slightly more vulgar conversation which goes on discreetly in the background without ever breaking in?

MARIEN: You could stop being beastly to Joan.

(Pause. Suddenly ROBERT gets up and goes and sits precariously on the side of Joan's chair.)

ROBERT: I'm now going to charm her.

(He pours out some champagne for her.)

We all have difficulties with life . . . I'd like to make love to you in a bath of the stuff.

(Pause. He drinks and leans over her purposefully.)

In the forest of the mind, Joan, above, the treetops of occupation and the parakeets of conversation with their brightly coloured plumage, there lurk the carnivorous mammals of neurosis which feed off the soft doe-eyed deer when they come to drink at the waters of innocence and inexperience. The forest stretches for ever, I am a big tiger with a mouth full of credit cards, honed to razor sharpness.

(He starts to get off and go back to his own seat.)

So watch it.

(Suddenly a complete change. Goes to door of tent and stands by it with a heroic pose.)

ROBERT (stiffly): I am going in for a while. I may be some time.

(Disappears inside the tent.

Pause. Then within.)

Read to them, Mack. They'll get bored. They mustn't get bored. Fill their silly heads with nonsense.

MARIEN (to GALE): I want to talk to you about Robert.

GALE: No —

MARIEN (to GALE): In private —

GALE: We've said *everything*.

MARIEN: Come on —

ROBERT (within): Let me hear you read to them −

   (MARIEN gives up and GALE and she turn a rather restless attention to MACK.

   MACK gets a small book out of the hamper, and opens it. Glares at his audience belligerently.

   They compose themselves in a resigned way.)

MACK (he can hardly read at all): Fr-o-m

   (Pause.)

   T-hugh-eee

GALE (helpfully): The?

MACK: From the.

   (Pause.)

GALE (gets up and looks over his shoulder. Helpfully): Where are we?

   (MACK points out a piece on the page.)

GALE: Moment −

MACK (dully, hating it all): Moment.

ROBERT (within): Don't help him anyone.

GALE: This is ridiculous.

ROBERT: Smack him if he gets it wrong.

GALE: For pity's sake − why are you trying to humiliate him?

ROBERT: If he wants to learn he'll have to sweat for it −

GALE (nerve-ends screaming): Oh − God!

MACK (looks up pathetically): I do − I do want to learn − I didn't have a chance at school −

   (ROBERT re-emerges with his suit on. Goes and stands over MACK, who cringingly takes up the book again.)

ROBERT: Read to them you miserable budgeon. You dull greasy member of the working class. You illiterate. You criminal industrial abortion.

   (Cuffs him on the head with his open palm.)

   Learn or not learn, you'll sweat for it −

GALE: Really, Robert! It's too difficult!

ROBERT: Education −

   (Cuffs MACK.)

   Is like putting on a pair of trousers −

   (Cuffs him again. MACK cringes.)

   It doesn't matter −

(Cuff.)

Which leg you put in first —

(MACK cringes and snivels: ROBERT goes and sits down, stretches out his legs.

Pause.)

The cloudless weather of that September and October need not be dwelt on further: it is a fact in history.

MACK (reads, rather faster): Commun-ism deprives no man of the power to appro —

ROBERT (swiftly prompting): Appropriate —

MACK: — the products of sock-iety, all it does is to depr-iv him of the pow-er to —

(Pause.)

ROBERT: Subjugate.

MACK: — the labour of others by me-ans of such appro-

(Pause.)

ROBERT: We'll leave it there.

(MACK lays the book aside.)

We'll continue after luncheon. Let us now continue with the great feast of life.

(The meal continues. Sotto voce requests for salt, mustard, napkins.)

GALE (after some time): Yeats must be buried near here.

JOAN: No, he's buried at Drumcliff.

MARIEN: Joan, could you tell us — those upended stones in the bays near Westport —

JOAN: Burials from the great famine.

ROBERT: Dead paddies. Hmm . . .

JOAN: The tombs have no names.

ROBERT: What were they doing? Standing in the queue for America?

JOAN: They died of hunger.

ROBERT: Doesn't do much for a culture if you can't remember their names.

JOAN: The Church prays for their souls.

(Pause.)

MACK: I think I'll just pop along and see if the car's all right Mr Martin.

(Stands.)

ROBERT (his mouth full): Oh?

MACK: There were some tinkers up the road. Don't want them — you know
... running their hands all over it.

ROBERT (as MACK goes out): Nasty, nasty tinkers. Who don't live like us.

(MACK exits.)

ROBERT: D'you read, Joan?

JOAN: Of course.

ROBERT: You could read to us. Stop Marien and I being beastly to each
other.

(GALE gets up, picks up her things and goes into the tent.)

ROBERT: Gale — what are you doing?

GALE: I'm going to change.

ROBERT: Why?

GALE: I just don't think we're going to get much bathing done.

ROBERT: No.

(GALE goes off.

ROBERT, JOAN, MARIEN in the remainder of the meal.)

MARIEN: The chauffeur.

ROBERT: I was looking forward to seeing you.

MARIEN (dignity, restraint): What are you doing with the chauffeur, Robert.
Are you trying to hurt me.

ROBERT (reasonable): Really, you just can't play straight bat to questions
like that.

MARIEN: What is your relationship?

ROBERT: Experimental buggery.

JOAN (embarrassed): Woud you like me to leave?

ROBERT (ingenuous): Joan, I had forgotten you were there. Take some
books — go down to the river and brood on its limpid whirls. There's a
good girl.

(JOAN is upset by all this pushing around. ROBERT gives her a handful
of books and an open bottle of champagne.)

The ingredients of a lovely afternoon.

(Her arms are full. He kisses her on the cheek.)

We own the universe —

(Turns her round.)

Think about spaceship earth and all who sail in her.

(Gives her a push and she goes off; he sits down facing MARIEN.)

MARIEN: The chauffeur.

ROBERT: He's ideal.

(Throughout the following action MARIEN and ROBERT's conversation continues. It is an agonising conversation and should be carried at an agonising pace.

Behind, around and above it, GALE's dream starts to take shape. These events are complementary and simultaneous.)

GALE'S VOICE OVER (recorded): This is Gale. Gale went to the only bush for miles around to change again. The day was warm. Staring into the earth she fell asleep. Robert and Marien droned on in the distance, trying to reassemble their lives. Both of them shell-shocked, the padded rooms beckon. Gale moved from the waking world into the madhouse of sleep, for her nine-hundredth dream about a swan. Perhaps this time it would be different.

(Burst of music from *Swan Lake*. MARIEN and ROBERT's light fades.

On another podium GALE comes on and rapidly puts on a ballerina's costume. She then poses, statuesque.)

MARIEN: I'm very worried. Can you afford him.

ROBERT: I don't run my life like a corner-shop.

MARIEN: Is that why it's such a fight to get money out of you each month?

ROBERT: No.

MARIEN: Are you having an affair with him?

(Pause.)

ROBERT: Travel's not what it was.

MARIEN: It won't last.

ROBERT: I paid for his driving to be civilised and it's spreading to the rest of his character. I think. And I won't have to pay him alimony.

MARIEN: I think you ought to see a psychiatrist.

ROBERT: Oh?

MARIEN: Seriously Robert I think you are going mad.

ROBERT: Typical right-wing response. It's perfectly normal. It's even legal.

MARIEN: Yes but you're doing it as an exhibition!

(Two gorillas emerge very slowly from a huge eyeball in the corner of the theatre. They help each other through, out of the optic nerve, then stand up. They bring a wind-up gramophone with a large horn.

[NB: If this is done in a proscenium theatre they should come through a trap.]

They are sharing a private joke with each other. They laugh silently, and constantly shush each other, fingers on mouths.

One of them winds the gramophone up with much pantomime palaver, and the other selects a record and puts it on.

It starts to play softly under MARIEN and ROBERT's desultory conversation. Dixieland rendition of 'Black Bottom'.

They listen to the conversation with glee.)

ROBERT: Where's Gale gone?

MARIEN: Gone to change.

(Calls.)

Gale!

(The GORILLAS take fright. They take the record off and rush back to the eyeball, but GALE does not move.)

GALE (serenely): I'm still asleep.

(The GORILLAS set up the gramophone again with much relief, wiping of brows.)

ROBERT: She's so young. Still.

MARIEN: She'll never make up her mind about anything.

ROBERT: She's cleverer than you are, she just doesn't know where to put it.

MARIEN: She's permanently immature.

ROBERT: I suppose that means we've had a mature relationship. She could lead a richer life if she used it properly.

MARIEN: She won't. She doesn't want anything badly enough.

ROBERT: She'll blossom and return to that great finishing school in the sky. She's very lucky, she doesn't have this self-destructive urge.

MARIEN: She isn't living, she's waiting. And if she doesn't change, she'll die doing just that. It's a waste.

ROBERT: She's not poor, she's attractive, she'll have children, friends, her life will be rounded out, she'll have a wonderful time in life's evening . . .

MARIEN: She'll sit it out.

(The GORILLAS push on a huge swan, the size of a donkey at least, and park it just by GALE. They invite her to mount it. One demonstrates. He sits behind neck and the other does an enthusiastic pantomime wank.)

GALE: No I won't. It tickles.

(The second GORILLA draws a full-size cardboard cut-out of ROBERT, out of the tail. Puts it so that the neck of the swan is like a huge penis between his legs.)

GALE: The answer is still no.

(They boo GALE, and blow raspberries. Disappointed, they pack up the gramophone, put it and the cut-out on the swan, and push them off.

The light slowly fades. The music has stopped. The GORILLAS walk slowly through the picnic. As the lights come up again. Then they exit. JOAN re-enters with the books and an empty champagne bottle.)

JOAN: Can I come back now?

ROBERT: Let's start the afternoon again. Joan, your afternoon will go uniquely: chicken, champagne, river, chicken, champagne, river —

JOAN: I'm not hungry thanks.

(GALE comes back.)

MARIEN: Have you changed, Gale?

GALE: No. I'm hungry.

ROBERT: Good for you, Gale, have some chicken.

GALE (flatly): I don't like chicken.

ROBERT: (still effusive) Champagne!

GALE (flatly): Reminds me of semen.

ROBERT: What's wrong with that?

GALE: I'll have some.

(GALE and JOAN sit down again.)

ROBERT (pouring): In one account of the Bloomsbury group, their emancipation from Victorian ideas of morality dated from the time Lytton Strachey pointed at a stain on Vanessa Stephen's dress, and said — 'Semen?' — raising his eyebrows.

(Pause.)

It brought the house down. Great punch-line.

(Pause.)

Of course, they were never the same again.

JOAN: Some people will do anything for a laugh.

ROBERT: Right on the button, Joan.
I hope somebody tells me when I get my punch-line.

(Pause.)

No jokes. Not in our lives.

MARIEN: Where's Mack?

JOAN: He went to the car.

ROBERT: He sits in the car and eats marzipan.

MARIEN: Extraordinary.

ROBERT: It's his version of affluence.

MARIEN: What *must* his teeth be like?

ROBERT (satisfaction): Like a row of bombed houses.

JOAN: Won't he ever go to the dentist if they hurt?

ROBERT (as intransigent as if they were his own): No.

MARIEN: The poor lamb.

ROBERT: He doesn't mind . . . he thinks he leads a wonderful life . . . he doesn't need our happy mouths . . . he's made good . . . but we've got nowhere else to go and so we're all afraid of our teeth . . . First they go, then we go . . . really, they just drop out first, why worry . . . oral hygiene probably makes for great unhappiness . . . let 'em rot . . . why worry . . . we're going to die anyhow, but until we do, we're in the great stream of life, getting richer and richer . . . the barriers between classes, countries are crap really . . . England, Ireland, one day . . . it'll be all like . . .

(Pause.)

California.

(Pause.)

There's our freedom.

(Pause.)

Many years ahead, and far away.

(Enter MACK from behind.

His mouth is bleeding: he has a steering-wheel tied round his neck, and his hands are tied.

They all turn.)

MARIEN: Oh no!

(MARIEN goes to MACK, and helps him to a chair, and starts to take the steering-wheel off.)

MARIEN: You poor lamb!

GALE: I feel sick . . .

(MACK grunts and weeps.

MARIEN holds his head.)

MARIEN: Oh Mack!

(Looks at his face. Without turning.

MARIEN looks inside his mouth.)

MARIEN: Where's all this blood coming from – is it internal?

(MACK shakes his head.)

Your mouth?

(MACK nods.

ROBERT goes to look in the tent and then comes back to where he was before.)

He's had a little bit of his tongue cut off — my God, the brutes . . .

(JOAN comes forward and cleans up his face, spitting on a handkerchief.)

JOAN: We'll have you cleaned up in no time.

MARIEN (testing for broken ribs): Breathe in . . . no sharp pains?

(MACK shakes head. JOAN has cleaned most of the blood off his face.

It's not so bad as they thought. Everybody starts to relax.)

ROBERT (at large): I'm not going into the tent.

MARIEN (absently): That's all right, I think the worst is over.

ROBERT (firm public statement): I am not going into the tent. Because there are two devils in the tent.

(Pause.)

I am not going in there because they will turn the canvas round and trap me.

MARIEN: What are you talking about?

ROBERT: They need my electricity. There's a little tap in my genitals which they can turn and the virtue will leave me. At this moment the air round here will soak up virtue instantaneously.

(They all stare at him.)

I know what you want me to do.

(He kicks the chair out of the way and goes into the tent.

A second later, the tent starts to writhe alarmingly.

GALE and MACK both start to laugh.

The tent falls.

ROBERT knocks over the table as well.)

ROBERT (within): You cunts! Don't you come near me! Well we can't stay here if *that* sort of thing goes on. Fucking barbaric peasants! I'll crucify your children for this!

MARIEN: Robert . . .

(ROBERT, tousled, reappears in the ruins of the tent.)

ROBERT: They took me in a flying saucer. Look down and you can see the whole of spaceship Earth. Our sweet planet which we have inherited. And they said, your riches will break you apart and you will finish your life in squalid poverty, and sickness. So if that is the future, then it won't be like California. Not like California at all.

out of sight.

The lights immediately come up at the end of HANFSTANGL's story to show the interior of GALE's London flat, which is a large first-floor room with french windows leading out on to a balcony.

Stage left an entrance to the kitchen through red, white and blue plastic drapes. Upstage left a double bed under the window. Next to it midstage, against the wall, is a table with a telephone and a stool or pouffe, stage left the french windows. Extreme stage left there is no exit apparent, the end of the room a jumble of unsuitable furniture, cheap thirties armchairs, contrasting strongly with the fitted drawers and louvred cupboard doors with the unmistakable look of a nasty yet professional conversion job.

The flat is the model for affluence gone sour. It has no particular style. There are dirty plates and cups everywhere, perched on every available extrusion.

The drawers are all throwing their contents out on the floor in the classic burgled pattern, the lower ones completely out, the top ones partially out.

One of the walls is mauve, another is red oxide.

There are sundry notices pinned on them, mostly in handwriting illegible to the audience. One visible notice is the front page of the *Daily Express* for 25 November 1972 which says MARTIN BORMANN ALIVE.

As the lights come up, GALE is asleep in the bed, as is MACK. JOAN is asleep on the balcony.

The door out of sight in the kitchen slams. GALE sits up in bed like a jack-in-a-box and looks round wildly.)

MARIEN's VOICE (from the kitchen): Oh! This is monstrous! How disgusting!

(GALE immediately leaps out of bed and puts on a crumpled long white flannel dressing-gown over pants, but no bra.

She swiftly collects three dirty saucers and mugs, then her initiative grinds to a halt and she stands in the middle of the room, momentarily nonplussed.

Pause.

MARIEN makes something of an entrance through the plastic strips, which are dealt with briskly. She is wearing a blue suit trimmed with white edging, and a blue closely-woven raffia hat.

Formidable. We see what she is carrying before her: it is a partially unwrapped, partially used half pound of butter on a plate.)

MARIEN: Ugh! This is rancid. I don't know how you can bear it — with this around, it's a wonder you can bring yourself to eat at all. Horrid.

(Pause. The actors begin to disperse. Then, sudden fade as they move.

Sound cue, Jagger, 'Memo from Mr Turner'. Followed by Grace Slick singing 'Chauffeur'.)

ACT TWO

The audience, summoned from the bar by the GORILLAS, start to sit down again. With the house lights still on, the GORILLAS come forward to address them.

GORILLA 1: All life is a tension between sex and death. Men long for one or the other all the time. They are the ultimate yearnings. Because, most of the time, neither of these ultimate urges is being achieved, men find it necessary to build civilisations to try and cover over these basic urges.

(And now they both start talking separately to different parts of the audience at the same time.)

GORILLA 1: The pleasure principle. What we really want at the bottom of it all is to have a good time, a really good time.

But it isn't easy to have a good time nowadays. You can't make love to everybody, all the time, so there are bound to be disappointments in life . . . But you can have a good time some of the time . . . If you don't go too far.

I hope you're enjoying yourselves. I hope you're getting pleasure. That's *our* pleasure principle. You know it makes sense. Stay with us. Don't make mistakes. Quietly to the grave.

GORILLA 2: At the bottom of it all we want to have the best time of all, and in practical terms we always settle for less. We always frustrate those sudden urges. Tonight, the middle way, a little pleasure. Not too much of anything, because in this world you lose it all that way, you end up unhappy, or dead . . .

That's *our* pleasure principle. No extravagant responses, please, from you. Don't slash the seats. Don't piss in the stalls. It may be less rewarding, but you're in civilisation, you've got to sit back for the moment and enjoy the view. Have fun. Nobody's digging anybody's grave tonight. No lunatics in the audience tonight I hope. No . . . unbalanced persons . . . we don't want anybody to go too far. Don't try to fuck *everybody*. Don't kill yourself trying to take over the world.

(When GORILLA 1 has finished his speech, he starts speaking GORILLA 2's, and when 2 has finished his he goes on to 1's.

At the end, one GORILLA jumps into the other's arms and says as they go off.)

GORILLA 1: And now, to finish the interval, a cautionary tale about someone who went too far —

(They exit. The house lights stay on.)

VOICE: Ernst Hanfstangl was a contemporary of T. S. Eliot at Harvard, and was for many years close to Hitler.

HANFSTANGL VOICE (elderly, German-American accent): My wife said, Putzi, that fellow is a neuter. What he was doing when he made his speeches, was making love to the whole of Germany, because he was impotent the only outlet for this enormous nervous energy, was oratory.

And there is no doubt, he was a genius, within the narrow provincial vision that made him think of the world as one big sportpalatz. But his sexual energies were perverted and twisted because they could find no outlet. He took beautiful actresses out for the night: in the morning, they would give the thumbs-down.

(The house lights start to go down.)

When his earliest putsch at the Feldenhalle failed, he was in my house when the police came. I had fled to Austria. He took his revolver and said, this is the end, I will never let these swine take me. I will shoot myself first. And my wife — one of the few ju-jitsu holds I had taught here — I'll show you — give me your hand.

(The house lights are extinguished.

The set is window stage right, french window stage left.

The orange light behind comes up, suggestive of a sodium-lit street at night.

No more lighting for the moment.

As HANFSTANGL continues his story, a figure in a high peaked cap, long coat, is silhouetted crossing stage right to left, with the silhouette on the windows.

It pauses outside the french windows where it is in full silhouette, and raises the gun to its head, level with its temple.

The figure remains like that in tableau for the rest of the speech.)

HANFSTANGL (continuing without a break): — and she disarmed him. She threw the revolver into a bowl of flour we kept in the attic.

Hitler was in love like a mooncalf with my wife, and when they had put him in prison he wanted to follow the example of the Sinn Fei and go on hunger-strike — my wife sent a message to him, she had prevented him from committing suicide in order to let him starve death. This advice from a beautiful woman turned the scale and called it off.

When he was in jail, surrounded and his mind poisoned by his c the worst sort of provincial anti-semites, I went to see him with son. He had a marvellous way with children and Egon adored there was never any sign of his private life having a sexual out everybody is essential and normal.

(The figure behind the french window suddenly drops the g

Horrid.

(She tips it into the wastepaper basket.)

GALE: Hey! This is the living-room.

MARIEN (brandishing the plate under her nose): How long d'you think this has been sitting there?

GALE: Why couldn't you use the rubbish bin in the kitchen?

MARIEN: It's not there.

(Surveys the room.)

Have you been burgled?

GALE: Well I never touched the rubbish bin in there.

MARIEN: This — is — different — to when you went away?

GALE: The window catch is broken.

MARIEN (hunting for the telephone directory): You'll be burgled again before you can turn round. Where's the Yellow Pages? As a present I'll order you a carpenter.

GALE: The phone doesn't work.

MARIEN: — and a telephone engineer —

GALE: They sent one round to cut it off.

MARIEN (takes this in): I can see why you jumped at the chance of a holiday.

(GALE gets back into bed without removing the dressing-gown.)

Where are Joan and Mack?

GALE: They're here.

MARIEN: What did they have to eat last night?

GALE: We all went without.

(Pause.)

I sent a taxi out with some money for fish and chips and it didn't come back.

MARIEN: Gale —

GALE (lights cigarette with ostentatious carelessness): C'est normal.

MARIEN: Now I don't want to —

GALE: Je m'en fous.

(Pause. Gets down further into the bed.)

It's so *early.*

MARIEN (her attention turned to the bed): There's *blood* on these sheets. You really are a little *slut*, Gale. What the trustees would say —

GALE (indignant): It's not me. It's Mack.

MARIEN: He's menstruating irregularly as well?

GALE: His mouth still bleeds sometimes.

MARIEN (pursuing the matter to the bitter end): Why's he done it in your bed.

(Pokes the sleeping MACK.)

Who's that then?

GALE: Leave him alone will you, you nosey old bag.

MARIEN (inquisitorial): And where's Joan.

GALE (flatly): On the balcony.

MARIEN: You put her out!

GALE: It's very warm.

MARIEN: Have you been sleeping with Mack?

GALE: He can't get to sleep at night. They only cut a tiny bit of his tongue out, but it's so sensitive, it always feels much bigger than it is.

(MARIEN sits down on MACK by mistake. MACK sits up with a startled grunt.

MARIEN gets off. Neither GALE nor MARIEN take any notice of MACK and he lies down again slowly.)

MARIEN: Why couldn't Joan sleep with him?

GALE (impish): I don't mind sleeping with him — and you know what these young Irish girls are like — probably wouldn't take precautions —

(Joan appears at the french windows blearily, wrapped in a sleeping-bag.)

MARIEN: I thought you were frigid.

GALE: Well some of the time I *am*.

MARIEN: Was this one of your on days?

GALE: I wasn't fucking him!

(Pause.)

MARIEN: I'm going to fix up to see Robert this afternoon. D'you want to come?

GALE: Poor Robert. Yes.

MARIEN: He's never been poor before, but he will be if he has his way. I'll come back and tell you when we can go.

GALE (from deep in the bed): Thank you coz.

MARIEN: Are you going to get up and tidy this place up?

GALE: Oh God . . .

(She gets out of bed and goes to the gramophone.)

MARIEN (helpfully): Really Gale, marriage is the only thing that will get you out of this.

GALE: I've lived with three men and it just doesn't suit me.

MARIEN: You didn't form a permanent relationship with them! That's why there are three. Anyhow I must go.

(She exits.

GALE puts a record on the gramophone.

Bach's version of 'Comfort ye, comfort ye my People'. Solo tenor.

She looks round, then goes off to the kitchen. JOAN still stays in one place by the french windows. She listens happily to the music.

GALE comes back with an electric kettle slopping water. She pulls the gramophone out of the socket, and puts the kettle in instead.

The gramophone dies miserably, the turntable running down.)

JOAN: You could do that in the kitchen.

GALE: There's such a *mess*. I forget where the socket is. I can't get to it anyhow.

JOAN: How is Robert?

GALE: Well I said we were going to see him this afternoon.

JOAN: He won't be well for some time you think?

GALE: I doubt it. It doesn't look like it.

JOAN: I ought to be getting a job then.

GALE: Stay here for what it's worth . . .

JOAN: I wouldn't mind coming inside tonight, what with the dew — and *people* — kept stepping over me!

GALE: That must be the burglars!

JOAN: Gracious!

GALE: I *knew* I used to have a television in that corner.

JOAN: We could have been murdered in our beds . . .

(Slight pause.)

And did Mack spend a quiet night.

GALE: I think he's still alive.

(JOAN comes into the room.)

He kept on rolling on top of me.

JOAN: Oh —

(GALE pulls the covers off the bed. There is MACK, fully dressed and still in his chauffeur's uniform, totally asleep.)

GALE: Every time he woke me up I gave him another two Mogadon. Come on Mack, you lazy old turd, time to go to hospital.

JOAN: He's got his clothes on still.

(She comes over.)

GALE: Not for want of trying.

JOAN: Let's have a look at his mouth.

(They pull MACK up between them and force his mouth open. He is still asleep. He half snores.)

JOAN (peering in): It's but a tiny piece, no bigger than a baby mushroom. When he was bleeding, I thought he was dying.

(She pulls him off the bed.)

JOAN: Come on, Samson, get in there and wash your face.

(MACK stumbles into the kitchen and disappears.)

Why did you tell Marien you slept with him?

GALE: I did sleep with him! I just wouldn't let him take his trousers off, that's all. At the moment his kissing isn't all that hot either.

JOAN: Can I put that record on again?

GALE: Yes of course.

JOAN: I love sacred music next to my heart.

(She unplugs the kettle and the gramophone starts up again immediately: 'Comfort Ye'.)

GALE (sits): We *must* get you a job. Unless you want to go back.

JOAN: There's no going back.

GALE (absently): That's the stuff.

(Pause.)

Joan, will you comb my hair please? I'll do yours.

JOAN: I'll get my brush out —

(A dull explosion in the kitchen. MACK walks into the room backwards. His clothes are smoking.

He falls over the gramophone, which dies in earnest this time.)

JOAN (redundantly): Oh! But he's on fire!

GALE (without moving): Quick! Put him out!

(MACK lies there smoking over the gramophone.)

JOAN: He's too heavy to lift —

GALE (agonised): No! Put him *out.*

(JOAN pours water from the just disconnected kettle over MACK who stops smoking and starts to steam instead. He yells, pitifully.)

GALE: That's *hot*, Joan.

(JOAN keeps pouring.)

Oh dear, I should have told him about the pilot light . . .

JOAN: We might have all been burnt in our beds . . .

(MACK leaps up and away from the punitive kettle.)

GALE: Is he out?

JOAN: Almost —

GALE: We'll have to get him out of here — it's no place to be accident prone in.

(Scribbles a note.)

Please-direct-to-Thomas' Hospital.

(To JOAN.)

Have you got any change?

JOAN: Irish money —

GALE: The two-bob bits fit in the ticket machines —

JOAN (putting money in MACK's free hand): Here.

(GALE gives him the note and they thrust him out through the door.

They come back into the room rather more relaxed.)

JOAN: Won't he be robbed of all he has if he's dumb in the streets?

GALE: He comes from Hackney.

JOAN: I thought London was getting just like New York.

(She finds a small gaily-wrapped parcel. Reads the label.)

'To Gale with lots of love from Lesley'

(Gives it to GALE.)

GALE: Christ I'd forgotten about that.

(She opens it. JOAN finds a comb and comes and stands behind her, worried.)

JOAN: What is it?

GALE (reads): It's a Personal Vibrator, ideal for neck massage etcetera.

JOAN: Some people keep their necks in funny places. It looks like a thing to me.

GALE: Dear Lesley. She thinks of everything.

(She turns it on and puts it on a tray on the floor.)

GALE (watching it gyrate in front of her): What is the attitude of the

Catholic Church towards personal vibrators?

(Pause.)

JOAN: Why aren't you married?

GALE: I find it impossible. I'll start again. I find it impossible to have a relationship which extends beyond mere social function.

JOAN: You haven't met the right man.

GALE: I don't think there is a right man.

JOAN: Shall I pop out and get some breakfast?

GALE (disturbed): I feel a novel coming on.

JOAN: It'll be good for you. It'll give you something to do when I'm out.

(JOAN grabs her bag and runs out. GALE is standing undecided in the middle of the room.

The kitchen door slams.

GALE picks up the vibrator.)

GALE (thoughtfully): How Wilhelm Reich
Vould have leiched
Ein Motor-beich . . .

(She throws it through the door, hard and gracefully as possible.

Cue for blackout.

Suddenly, flashing lights and dashing waves, storm sounds, very loud — but not loud enough to drown the speech of the GORILLAS, who come in again. This time they are wearing sou'westers. They swing down from the podium in a shower of hurricane lamps.)

GORILLA 1: Avarst there!

(Megaphone.)

Lash the bo's'n to the stern!

GORILLA 2 (swinging down after him, megaphone throughout): Avarst there!

GORILLA 1: Stormy seas!

GORILLA 2: She founders!

GORILLA 1: Fire the distress rockets!

GORILLA 2: Fire the distress rockets!

GORILLA 1: Let off the maroons!

GORILLA 2: Let off the maroons!

(They bring on the swan, like a couple of worthy coxswains.)

GORILLA 1: Or the dice will fall where they may!

GORILLA 2: Where they may!

GORILLA 1 (goes to GALE): Action lady, the boat is sinking. you must board our small craft. There is a perpetual storm in the universe.

(They reel about the stage.)

You must join the monstrous regiment of married women!

GORILLA 2: Married women!

GALE (from the bed): I don't want to.

GORILLA 1: If you haven't got a fella, we'll find you a fella! Get on the swan and we'll take you to one!

(The storm continues.)

GALE: I don't want a fella!

GORILLA 2: Wilhelm Reich, he say, it's good to get your end away!

GALE: All right!

GORILLA 1: We can't stay any longer, or we shall be dashed to pieces against the eternal rocks!

GALE: All right then, you get me a fella!

(The GORILLAS are overcome with joy and bound all over the stage. They push the swan off and have an orgy of anticipation in the continuing storm.)

GORILLA 1: Tonight's the night! She's gonna get a poke tonight!

GORILLA 2: She's gonna get her rocks off tonight!

GORILLA 2: Tonight's the night!

GORILLA 1: She's going to punt her muff tonight!

(Etc.)

GORILLA 2: Tonight's the night!

(Etc. Etc.

They dance off, deliriously happy with each other.

The lights go back to normal. GALE is still lying on the bed where she fell at the beginning of the scene.

JOAN is in the doorway, apparently pregnant. GALE sees this.)

GALE: Oh my God!

(JOAN gives a wriggle and a shower of fruit falls out on to the floor.)

This is going too far!

JOAN: The wee man would have nothing to do with my money, so I put them down my front as I was passing the time of day with him.

GALE: You stole from the man who gave you fruit!

JOAN: He gave me nothing, he just wouldn't take the money, he kept saying, 'It's no good with a harp on it.'

(She picks up the fruit.)

GALE (shocked): I've never stolen anything in my life!

JOAN: There's plenty of fruit on those stalls.

GALE: Robbing the working classes —

JOAN: I *am* the working classes, I thought you said.

GALE: Of course, I do so beg your pardon.

JOAN: And I've no money that they'll take, so I'm doubly oppressed.

GALE: In principle I'm delighted you're liberating yourself from the stuffy old capitalist system, I just don't want the flat full of stuffy old policemen.

JOAN: Is this flat yours then?

GALE (instantly embarrassed): Well it's a bit complicated, Mummy set up this trust, and the trust undertakes to provide mortgage rates if they are lower than a short-term lease on a furnished flat would be over a given period.

So in a very roundabout way, yes. Only because it's cheaper in the long run. And it's a very tiny flat.

JOAN: Will the trustees let you have a bigger one when you're married?

GALE: Oh yes, they're not mean, quite the opposite, rosy-cheeked philanthropists, to a man: it's just that I do believe one should live frugally. And —

(Pause.)

I won't ever get married so the question doesn't arise.

JOAN (alarmed at the steely tone): You sound as if you'll be glad when it's over.

GALE: The extrovert gets along better in the first half of life, the introvert in the second.

(Pause. MARIEN comes in.)

I look forward, with intense anticipation, to the second half.

MARIEN: Robert's very ill. I talked to Jameson who's always looked after him and he said he was prepared to serve him with a 72-hour restraining order but needed an impartial account of the incident: I can't sign him in like I did in Ireland.

GALE: When that expires?

MARIEN: If there's any trouble we can ship him back to Ireland because the order still stands there.

GALE: You want me to go and say he ought to be locked up?

MARIEN: Jameson's being very weak about the whole thing — wants another account of the incident, social workers won't commit him themselves – they've got all sorts of ideas about freedom. But the most important thing as far as I can see is to put him inside where he can't get at his bank account. That's the thing I'm worried about. You may have to exaggerate. I did, God forgive me.

GALE: What's he doing?

MARIEN: Nothing, apart from a couple of incidents with young nurses. He's giving all his money away.

GALE: Well he would have got rid of it anyway.

MARIEN: At this rate, he'll never adjust to the shock. He'll spend all his money and kill himself at the end of the week.

GALE (thoughtfully): A new world speed record for middle age.

MARIEN: He doesn't know what he's doing. It may be his responsibility when he's sane, but ours when he's not. We *all* owe it to each other. If I went mad, I'd expect society to look after my interests while I was incapable of looking after them for myself.

GALE: He's not a danger to society now –

MARIEN: He will be when he's poor!

GALE: Maybe he's got tired of owning things. Perhaps he felt that ownership came between you.

MARIEN: I am sick and tired of your immature attitude towards property, Gale. In your case it's a lack of assertion of personality, which shows us everything you do.

(To JOAN, for want of better support.)

Do you know she won't even have a maid in here to tidy up?

JOAN (getting the wrong end of the stick): I don't mind doing it right now . . .

MARIEN: All right – so you feel it's wrong to exploit people. But there are people living in Camden Town who would leap at the opportunity to scrub your floor, and you could pay them handsomely for it and you'd both feel better.

(Her patience is exhausted.)

Really I don't know what to do with you Gale, you're so *dilatory*.

GALE (as always the supple defence): You don't have to do anything with me.

MARIEN: You've got more influence on Robert than any of us –

GALE: Balls.

MARIEN: If you wanted to you could persuade him –

GALE: I don't want to. I think he's doing the right thing.

MARIEN: If that's what you really think then you should give your flat and your money away.

GALE: There are several reasons why women should own property — chiefly their reduced earning power. And I'm not going to wash away my debt to society by trumping up commital orders with that drunk of a family doctor.

(MARIEN has had enough. Angrily and tearfully she turns to go.)

MARIEN: All right —

GALE: He doesn't like money because it keeps you apart. I should let him get rid of it if I was you — he obviously can't cope with having it —

(MARIEN goes out slamming the door.

GALE goes to the french windows and shouts after MARIEN.)

GALE (shouts): If you love Robert then you should still love him when he's poor.

MARIEN (off): Taxi!

(GALE comes in again. Pause.)

GALE: Let's eat.

(They start to leave, but she changes her mind.)

No. Let's go and get pissed, and pick up some rough stuff.

(JOAN and GALE exit eagerly.

The lighting stays the same for the moment.

Sound cue. Steve Miller Band, the middle of the track 'Song for our Ancestors'.

MACK enters, changed into something rather less baroque than the chuaffeur's uniform. He comes in through the french windows with another man.

They burgle the flat with great speed and thoroughness, taking the bed-clothes, the telephone, curtains and the carpet.

Everything goes out through the kitchen where one of them has opened the front door.

When they have finished, the set should look stripped. MACK and the 2ND BURGLAR go out through the kitchen, again with magical speed.

The lights outside the windows go down to evening.

The record stops.

The sodium lights come on in the street outside, and shine through the windows orangely.

Pause.

The sound of a taxi stopping outside.

This is the first time we hear ALKO's voice. It is authoritative, Mid-West, three parts drunk.)

ALKO's VOICE: Is that a pound note then?

(The sound of drunken people coming upstairs.

The door in the kitchen opens, flooding the area behind the plastic strips with light.)

GALE's VOICE: There are lots of mattresses –

(The sound of a tap being turned on.

ALKO belches monstrously.)

GALE's VOICE: Lucky that one got out.

ALKO's VOICE: Yeah, if it hadn't, it woulda tore a fresh asshole –

GALE: She's passing out again.

(Noise of a falling body on boards.

GALE comes in through the plastic strips.

Lights up on stage. GALE pirouettes round the stage, sings 'Some Enchanted Evening'.

ALKO comes in behind her.

He is a huge muscular American, in sweater and light-coloured trousers and sandals.

He carries an unconscious JOAN in his arms with some ease.)

ALKO: Is she always like this?

(GALE does not answer. She is staring round the room in disbelief.)

D'you have a bowl, Twinkletoes?

GALE (not listening): A bowl . . .

ALKO: She's going to be sick again.

(JOAN starts to retch and ALKO seizes the wastepaper basket and holds her head to it.)

ALKO: Here you are, you little bogtrotter.

GALE: I've been burgled . . . I've been so utterly burgled . . .

ALKO: There's a funny smell . . . like butter when it's gone off.

GALE (suddenly makes up her mind): Ha. Yes. I've been burgled. Good. My mind's made up.

ALKO: What?

GALE: For a moment I thought we were in the wrong flat. What a relief. Wonderful.

ALKO: Are you insured?

GALE: No! You see, it's all fat. Rubbish. When I die, I want to be found in a bare room, in a broken-down house, six weeks later, odourless, dessicated.

ALKO: There is a funny smell in here.

GALE: You see I don't want anything to do with the people who stole the stuff.

ALKO: Shouldn't you tell the police.

GALE: If there's a man going up the Charing Cross Road at this moment with a case full of dirty knickers and a colour television, he's welcome to them. Before Marien and I went to Ireland, there was a chair there, and I used to sit in it and cry. It's wonderful now, it's gone.

ALKO: What are you going to do now?

GALE: There's nothing, nothing I want to do. The only possible things I like doing is refusing to do things, like refusing to commit Robert. Marien's still in love with him you know. What do you think I should do?

(Pause.)

ALKO: The way you're going . . . I suppose you could try on a few grass skirts . . .

GALE: Do you believe in love?

ALKO: As the Rabbi said to the actress, it sure beats pork.

GALE: Do you think people, when they're in love, own each other?

ALKO (his brow furrows): Shit . . . Ah . . ! Dunno . . .

GALE: You see Marien has these desperately insecure old-fashioned ideas about property — perfectly natural for a woman of her age.

ALKO: Hey little girl, d'you like Jack Daniels?

GALE: No. Marien's a bitch sometimes. When she was in Ireland and Robert went mad, she committed him as his wife although technically she's divorced from him in this country — if you're married in Church in Ireland, it's for keeps. And then they come back here, and she's been lying to the doctors as if she owned him — but she must let him get rid of it — he must be free to do that; he's made money his neurosis.

The only thing that I know I own is my body, and then only because it's no use to anybody else.

ALKO (indicating himself): I hired this from Godfrey Davis.

(To her.)

Yours is nice.

GALE: Yes. Very good. It's very big isn't it.

(Pause.)

Do you feel you could admire my body without owning it? I'm called Gale. I'm very interested in psychology. Especially assumptions which have passed into the language. What's your name?

ALKO: Alko.

GALE: And what are you doing in England?

ALKO: I'm with four USAF teams that are touring Europe giving exhibition matches of American football to the Communist bloc, to try and raise our reputation a little for gamesmanship.

(Takes out a football shirt and holds it to himself.)

Now at an all time low.

GALE: Are you in the Airforce now?

ALKO: No I'm through.

GALE: How long are you staying?

ALKO: Well I made out an application to the Sorbonne to read eighteenth-century French history, which is my first love, but I don't know if it's gone through.

(GALE opens his case and pulls out some shoulder pads.)

The pads go here . . . and here . . .

(Shows her.)

There are also hip pads . . .

(GALE gets up suddenly and walks to the end of the room and turns.)

GALE: Will you put them on?

ALKO: What, now?

GALE (insistent): Please.

ALKO: Why?

GALE: Because.

(Firmly.)

It'd be nice.

(ALKO starts to change reluctantly.)

ALKO: Well I suppose it was a goodwill tour . . .

GALE (watching him): Good. Good.

ALKO: Do you want me to hum 'The Stars and Stripes'?

(GALE goes to the french window and plays with the lock.)

GALE: Played its part . . . never be the same again . . .

(She goes outside on to the balcony as ALKO continues to change. She sings.)

Dilly dilly
Dilly dilly
Come and be killed . . .

ALKO (changing): Oh mother earth, what a fool am I . . .

(GALE comes back into the room and is delighted with his progress.)

GALE: It's the real McCoy.

ALKO: That's my name.

GALE (disbelievingly): No . . .

ALKO: That's my name.

GALE (high as a kite): Oh how droll! Isn't life droll? It never treats people kindly but it sometimes is droll.

ALKO: That's not what Elvis said to his mother.

GALE: Tell me what Elvis said to his mother.

ALKO: He said, 'Mother, God has been good to us.'

(Pause. Suddenly, they both laugh.)

Is Joan going to die of hypothermia?

(He is now fully changed.)

GALE: We could cover her with curtains.

(ALKO puts his helmet on. Mugs outrageously, arms akimbo.)

GALE: Here —

(ALKO does a cod football routine, muttering incoherently, turns and kneels by GALE.

She climbs up and sits on ALKO's shoulders.)

ALKO (sings): With voices strong, we raise our song, fight on for victory — RA! RA! RA!

(ALKO goes to the curtains and stands while GALE picks them off the runner.

Pause.)

GALE: Are you going to make love to me?

ALKO: Have to take my hat off, first —

GALE (still taking down the curtains): Seriously . . .

ALKO: One of us is bound to be ticklish.

GALE: Seriously — what would you like?

ALKO: Where can we put the young colleen . . . in the bath?

GALE: We'll just have to be quiet.

ALKO (glum): People say that, and then it turns out like a hog-calling competition.

(GALE finishes taking down the curtains. ALKO lowers her to the ground.)

GALE: Why are you so worried?

ALKO: Oh . . . It's just that *normally*, one tends, statistically, if one is a white Anglo-Saxon Protestant, to clear other people off to bed before congress . . .

(GALE spreads the curtains over the sleeping JOAN, takes off her tights and dress and jumps under the curtains.)

GALE (firmly): I'm ready.

ALKO (confused): Call me an old fuddy-duddy . . .

(Walks about undecided.)

I've only just put this lot on.

GALE: Gerremoff.

(ALKO takes his sweater off.)

ALKO (gloomily): Oh boy . . .

GALE: Is that how you feel about things?

ALKO: Yes ma'am.

GALE: Leslie Fiedler thinks that all American males want to leave their wives and go and live with coloured boys. Is that true?

ALKO (deadpan): Yes ma'am.

GALE: What's your worry?

ALKO: I just been out-niggered.

(Pause. He gets into bed with most of his clothes on. Hands GALE an armour-plated jockstrap from his case.

GALE raps it with her knuckles.)

ALKO: You just hang on to that and we'll both be happy.

GALE (raps it again): What is it?

ALKO: My neutrino shield.

(The lights start to go down.)

GALE: What are neutrinos?

ALKO: They're not sure.

GALE: And are there many of them?

ALKO: They caught a few but they're not talking.

GALE: And does the shield stop them?

ALKO: They're not sure . . .

(Lights down to the sodium street lighting outside.

Pause.)

GALE: What's that?

ALKO (ironic pride): America . . .

(There is a long pause. The silhouette of MACK and another person at the windows, and they start to roll up the carpet in the room, coming in through the french windows.)

GALE (a note of strain): Alko — I think there's someone in the room!

ALKO: If we can just try to ignore diversions right now . . .

(Pause. MACK goes to the kitchen, where there is a hideous crash.)

GALE: It must be Mack, he's accident prone . . .

ALKO (hopefully): Perhaps it's a mouse.

GALE: Bigger than that — bigger than a rat —

ALKO (still hopeful): Super Rat?

(During this period while they are making love and MACK & Co. are emptying the flat, the lights change to what they were during GALE's 'dream'. Flashing light at the back and sound cue, Procol Harum, Salty Dog track of the Salty Dog LP, which fades with the lighting effects as MACK finishes and goes out slamming the door. Pause.

Then, very faintly, the noise of sawing.)

GALE: Is somebody *snoring*?

ALKO (sourly): Super Rat's dropped off.

(The light comes on.

Far stage left, a saw projects through the wall, sawing downwards and spilling plaster through at each stroke.

Pause.

ALKO puts on his football shirt and holding it discreetly over his privates gets out of bed to investigate the saw in the wall.

Stares at it.

Raps on the wall with his knuckles.)

GALE: It must be Mack. Tell him to go away.

ALKO (calls): Mack?

(Pause.

Then deliberately.)

Go away, this time you have gone too far.

GALE: Can't you pull it through and snap it off?

ALKO: It's covered in teeth for chrissake!

(Bangs on the wall with fist.)

Stop this silly nonsense immediately!

(Pause. He goes back and sits on the bed.)

GALE: What are you doing?

ALKO: I know when I'm licked.

(Takes off his shirt.)

I want whoever it is to realise they're interrupting an intimate scene.

(Puts on the helmet.)

GALE: They've got to saw three more sides before they can come through. We could ring the police . . .

ALKO: Super Rat's taken the phone.

GALE: It didn't work anyhow.

(The saw withdraws. There is a pause.

There are a few deep thumps as if the sawers were trying to get through.

The plaster board splits with a mighty crash and ROBERT, covered in plaster, falls through in a cloud of dust.

He is white all over. He wears hospital pyjamas.

He falls over in the room then stands up proudly and indicates the hole that he's made.)

ROBERT (gestures): The Rape of the Room.

GALE: Robert — ?

ROBERT (indicates hole again): Your dusty hymen, madam. I have abandoned my property and my respect for it. Prepare yourself for violation.

ALKO: Is *that* Robert?

ROBERT: Oh . . . there appears to be another homunculus in here before me. Does that mean that I shall have to take my little wriggly tail and go?

GALE: No Robert — don't go.

ROBERT: It's very bare in here. Are you moving down to the country? It's wonderful you know the freedom of choice which is open to the middle classes.

(Looks around.)

Last Night in the Old Home.

GALE: I've just been burgled.

ROBERT: Is this the first time for both of you? Captain Spock?

GALE: Don't be silly.

ROBERT: Has Captain Spock got a lock on his cock?

(GALE laughs. Pause.)

You could stop conventional burglars getting in you know, spyglasses, deadlocks, marbles under every window — but not me. Never stop me.

You do think I should be locked up don't you. You can't just go swanning round breaking into people's houses.

(Pause.)

Not unless you're a policeman . . .

When you go mad, you see, you break out of the tiny room where you've been living, and attempt to take over the universe again by storm, wicked puns and brute force. The ghostly surgeon operates on his own heart. I'll show you. Have you a penknife?

(They stare at him.)

The madness starts with burial. For years I pretend to be Robert Martin and it's a character who I have less and less sympathy for. There are lots of people like him. In a hundred and fifty years the whole world will be covered in the middle classes like gravy round a meatball.

. . . We have the *energy* of madness, but we consume ourselves because we despise the way we live now. My pathetic story is that I want out. Some people say that out is a very middle-class place. But people do change. I won't have to sit inside my car like a trussed turkey. Freedom. Yes? Madness. Well-defined social roles. White-coated doctors, struggling patients. I am mad, aren't I?

I mean, I came in by the wall, and I could so easily have used the window. Please — may I use your phone to ring for them to take me away — I'm a menace, it's a criminal matter at the very least.

GALE: They've taken the phone.

ROBERT: Could I trouble you to get up and call the police?

GALE: No.

ROBERT: Foiled again. Well what I'll do is tie you and Captain Marvel up with bare flex and jam it into the mains, and while you writhe, the searchlights train on the house. Marien — loudspeaker "Come back darling I still love you". Me — through another loudspeaker — "No".

I could have been a power for good, I could have wrestled with the world to change it for the better in cunning awys . . . But I've done it now, I've taken the jump . . .

They'll change me, they've got to change me. Keep the scapegoats quiet. I'm doing this for all of you. I'm doing this entirely on your behalf.

(Sits on the bed.)

We did nothing. We started no wars, we didn't love properly, we paid our taxes.

(JOAN is sat upon by ROBERT. She sits up with a startled cry.)

JOAN: Jesus and Joseph.

ROBERT: Joan. You're a lovely girl.

(He extends a trembling hand to her.)

JOAN: I'm going to be sick again I think.

(ALKO gives her the wastepaper basket. She puts her head in it, and retches.)

ROBERT (peers at her): Cast a cold eye, on meatballs, on gravy;

Diners, pass by.

Don't you recognise me Joan? I am Robert, that once thought you were an amusing little peasant. Underneath this coat of gypsum, my hair is white as snow. The right-hand side of my face is going up, the left-hand is going down. Better proof of a psychic volcano could I not give you were lava streaming out of my ears.

And you, presumably, are still an amusing little peasant.

JOAN (gombeen drunk): Who's dat?

ROBERT: Jesus, Joseph and Mary are the ghostly surgeons and they're going to bang eight trillion volts from ear to ear to try and get rid of a little bowler hat that they've found growing in the forebrain.

I'm thirsty.

(JOAN, ALKO and GALE look at him uncomprehendingly from the bed.)

ALKO (with ill grace): There's some Jack Daniels in my case.

ROBERT: If that's the best you can offer, I'm off . . .

(He peers in the hole.)

Can I get out through the front door, Gale.

(He turns as he reaches the plastic strips.)

You will look after her, Captain Spock, won't you. She's a very sweet, very lovely girl, and I've always wanted to do something with her . . . bite her arse . . . I don't know . . . the struggle with the alien world prevented me. In this case the world is played by my wife. The question of who fucks who has taken up so much time in everybody's lives . . .

(He suddenly breaks down.

MARIEN enters.)

Kiss me goodbye, Joan.

(He goes over and they kiss briefly.)

I'm sorry my nose is running, it's the Seconal.

(To MARIEN.)

You have just been cast as the world, but if you like you can play the universe.

(Picks up a piece of paper, prepares to wipe his nose on it.)

Is the cause of the distress a rogue gene, original sin, or the unhappy rich, Marien?

(He unwraps the paper and is about to blow his nose on it. Becomes engrossed.)

Tonight in the studio we have a middle-aged housewife, a university graduate, an Irish maid and a football player.

MARIEN: You've made a terrible mess of the wall, Robert.

ROBERT (laughs): A mess . . . We don't like mess do we. We must tuck the corners in. There was an old boy who sat in the corner of my club, having survived the First World War, the first mechanical apocalypse. And all he could say was – The *noise*! The *people*!!!

Come on Marien, let's flee from justice. That would hold us together, wouldn't it. We could go to Ireland, and live quiet as mice in the hills behind Cork and farm pigs –

(He steps towards her and stumbles. She holds him. They start to exit holding each other.)

Then one day, you could beat me to death with a rolling pin, to stop my everlasting going on and on at you . . .

(They exit. JOAN, ALKO and GALE watch from the bed. Sound cue 'La Donna e Mobile', followed by 'S'Oppressan' from *Nabucco*.)

ACT THREE

The Third Act is set in a tent belonging to the circus of Aeroplane Parker, a French circus owner. MARIEN and ROBERT are living in the tent. It is packed with old circus items round the perimeter of the stage.

Poles, harness, old lions' cages, elephants' howdahs, etc. Very obvious must be the swan used in the earlier acts, and anything else that might double as a theatrical prop and has been used already. So the abandoned circus looks like the junkyard of the mind.

One of the GORILLA's suits also hangs up prominently.

Overhead, sloping up towards the audience at an angle of forty-five degrees, is the canvas roof of the tent. It has a large hole in it midstage. It should be made clear in the design that this is the storage tent rather than the main ring. There are two hammocks slung between poles.

Very low lighting, hardly enough to show all this. MARIEN and ROBERT are behind a screen upstage left, and out of sight of the audience.

Through the back flap opening, a GORILLA suddenly walks forward and addresses the audience. The voice is heavily synthesised, on tape with lots of static, but quite quick. This GORILLA is all gold. He has a gold crown on. He has a large erection reaching up to the middle of his chest. This is gold. He has large breasts also. These are gold. He has catharnae disguised as large feet, also gold. He has a golden cloak.

He halts downstage. Kisses the tips of his fingers to the audience. Under one arm he has a humming spinning-top, on which are painted (as if it were a sphere) the countries of the world, as on a globe, with blue for the sea.

Over the static, which has died down to a low level now, is a swift majestic voice over. The golden GORILLA pumps up the spinning-top of the world, and gestures with the VOICE to the audience.

VOICE: I am a primal force. You and I keep the world going between us. I am everything you ever dreamed of. I have a message for you.

Gale's novel shall never be finished. Life goes on. Two years pass. Marien and Robert live in a circus tent. Gale and Alko live in Sittingbourne. They inhabit different galaxies. I have a message for you.

The universe contains several of everything.

(He leaves the top. Magically, a gold-painted aluminium ladder comes through the rent in the canvas and he goes and starts to climb up it and disappear.)

Love leads us all to strange places. There before you for your amusement, very quickly, is a history of your life upon the earth. For all of you. I have a message for you. It is − eel.

(He disappears. The spots go to the humming top. They stay on it till it falls over. Blackout. Sound cue: 'At the Hop', first few bars.

Lights up on the stage. Sickly brown and grey. An ugly light. It will not show anyone up to advantage.

ALKO pulls aside the flap of the opening at the back and peers in. He comes into the middle and stands and looks around. Then GALE does the same. They are both wearing smart, outdoorish sorts of clothes.

Very faintly, watery noises from behind the screen. ALKO and GALE, very ill at ease, look at each other then back at the screen.

The screen falls outward to reveal ROBERT sitting facing the audience, the wrong way round on a chair. MARIEN is washing his back.)

ALKO (sotto voce to GALE): Shall we wait outside?

ROBERT: Isn't it raining?

(Pause. Then JOAN comes in backwards through the flap pulling behind her a pram.

Pause.)

Hello Joan. What a surprise. I thought Gale disapproved of servants. How are you finding it in England?

JOAN (wrinkling her nose): Robert go on, you're not really living here.

(ROBERT gets up, wraps a towel round himself and walks off through the debris without saying a word.)

MARIEN (nervously): He'll see you all in a minute . . .

GALE (coaxing): Oh, coz −

(GALE and MARIEN run together and embrace. MARIEN bursts into tears.)

MARIEN: God I've missed you Gale − He says it's the only way, but I've missed you so much − You're looking terribly well −

(Wipes away tears.)

I'm a stupid old woman . . .

(Goes to JOAN and kisses her.)

Joan darling, so you're a *nanny* now, you look radiant −

JOAN (more shocked than anyone): Does Robert make you live here?

MARIEN: It is rather odd − but Robert met a French circus manager when he was in hospital, none of them could get work permits − they were going to start in Bradford as soon as the Common Market started − we were to look after their things for them, but they never came back so we stayed there − I don't know whether to be glad or sorry . . .

(Turns and embraces GALE again.)

And you've had a *baby*, oh God, you're so lucky — you are happy together aren't you? Say you're happy together.

GALE (pleasing her): Yes.

MARIEN: And your house? How is your house? Robert still won't have any possessions —

GALE: It's fine. D'you have a loo?

MARIEN: My dear, it's frightfully primitive.

(Leading her off.)

I'm so sorry about the mess . . .

JOAN (points to hammock): Who sleeps there?

MARIEN: I — we do — we had to move off the floor because of the rats . . .

(ALKO and JOAN are left alone on stage.

Pause.)

JOAN: Our pig lived better.

ALKO: Well it proves what I always said. The real enemy is poverty and always will be. What does he think he's doing? It's the wrong country for hermits.

JOAN: Alko — while we're on the subject of money. Of course I appreciate my keep and that, but I don't get much to send back.

ALKO: If I had it, Joan, I'd give it to you like a shot.

JOAN: Seriously, I've thought about it and I reckon I'm getting screwed. You can go on so long — I'm very fond of you and Gale and Posset — but I'm being screwed.

ALKO: My advice to you, honey, is to lie back and enjoy it.

JOAN (ignoring this): I don't have enough money to go to the cinema, or buy nice clothes, or go to London. Twelve quid a week and my keep is just *not enough.*

ALKO: I love it when you're angry.

(His arm round her shoulder.)

I really wanted to marry you, but I got confused on that one time and turned the wrong way in bed. We should try it again one day.

JOAN (breaking away): God you're a slimy bastard sometimes, Mr McCoy. I want another six quid a week.

ALKO: Tell you what. Would you like a . . . . televison set in your room.

JOAN: Separate to these negotiations, yes!

ALKO (frustrated patronage): Smartass.

(Pause.)

Look Joan, can I just work out the horrid existentialist mess of your National Insurance — right? — and then we can come to some sort of arrangement.

JOAN: Tonight.

ALKO: Well we're not staying here tonight.

JOAN: Isn't it awful?

ALKO: Listen beautiful Joan, here are the car keys — can you go and get the bottle of Teachers which is laying in the back.

JOAN (going out): It's raining, you bloody tyrant.

(She kicks him on the way out. ALKO catches her, puts her arm in a half nelson and slaps her on the arse.

Suddenly ROBERT reappears. He has a raggety clown's suit on. He also has a whistle round his neck. He takes it and blows it.)

ROBERT: Offside!

(JOAN exits glowering.)

ROBERT: Have you laid her yet? I mean, I wouldn't have thought that Gale was that enthusiastic a partner. More of a nibbler than a gobbler. She knows it. In her case it's worse because of her class conditioning and affluence. Gale's problem is not enough vulgarity whereas you are in full flight from it. Your child?

ALKO: What?

ROBERT: You're infuriatingly slow, Alko. What sort of education will you give it?

ALKO: The best I can afford.

ROBERT: And in twenty years time we can look forward to seeing someone lounging around mouthing anglicised versions of your platitudes. Are you glad the Vietnam war's over? I mean you fought in it. Along with all the other liberals in the western hemisphere, are you glad that your evil work is being undone?

(ALKO for the first time we see angry.)

ALKO: They never draft a man twice.

ROBERT: Civilisation. God preserve us from it.

(JOAN comes back in with a bottle.

ROBERT indicates ALKO.)

Give Sonny Liston a drink.

ALKO: You're fulla shit.

ROBERT: You're a very coarse person, Alko, but I'm sure you're a good man in a snowstorm.

(Then friendly.)

You're a Cartesian, you see. You've been brought up to think that your mind and the world are separate, but we're at the end of the Cartesian age. There is no division between ourselves and the world. Between miracles and feats of the imagination. You don't understand me. You don't understand what I'm trying to do here.

ALKO: You aiming for a child?

ROBERT: Marien wants a child. She can't have one, but that's her affair. I'll have a drink.

ALKO: Gale and I are very worried about you.

ROBERT: Gale's worried about Marien.

ALKO: Aren't you?

ROBERT (softly): Don't waste your time with that crap.

ALKO: What will you do if Marien has a child here?

ROBERT: That's not to do with me. I'm a full-time prophet. This place is on the convergence of two key lines. Like Glastonbury. The tent pole is 1,586 feet above sea level. If you do something with this number — I forget what — it turns into the number of the Great Beast of the Apocalypse. If we manage to stay here much longer, even Marien will start turning into a witch. Do you know, it's a dreadful trade, prophesy. Nostradamus got round the problem by writing out the next three hundred years all jumbled up — Completely incomprehensible: A stew of heraldic cartoons. We all come to balderdash in the end. I find it very difficult to be genuinely superstitious. A dreadful trade. I wouldn't do it if I hadn't exhausted the alternatives. Raging around the moors in the mist with a hard-on at my age. I ask you.

(He turns.)

Joan, give me a kiss.

(He gnaws at an indifferent JOAN's neck.)

Come and live with us instead, Joan.

JOAN: Oh no, I couldn't be three in a bed again.

ROBERT: Why so sour? Joan, you have youth, beauty, and a ready wit. You should be happy

JOAN (breaking away from ROBERT's ever increasingly audacious embrace): Well I would if I had a fair wage.

(ROBERT laughs loudly.)

It's not as if I'm free. I'm tied hand and foot here and my spending money isn't related to real prices at all, but I'm tied all the same. You choose to be married and have children — I couldn't make that choice because my family's dependent on me — I'm not free to be married and have children of my own — I get very poorly paid for being what I am — not much more than if I was still in Westport.

(ROBERT still laughing. GALE and MARIEN enter.)

ROBERT: And the punch-line is —

JOAN: So —

(Emphatically.)

I want six pounds a week more.

(ROBERT laughs.

This stops GALE and MARIEN in their tracks. JOAN has caught GALE's eye. GALE looks down.

Pause.)

GALE: Yes of course, I'm ashamed, we should have done this long ago — one didn't think of it —

(ROBERT laughs.

To ALKO.)

You know we have been underpaying her.

ALKO (angry): The sky's the limit now — a fortnight's paid holiday in Yugoslavia — that's two month's scotch ration right off — you just give it away because you feel guilty — where's it going to stop?

(At large.)

You have a family — and it's like standing under a shower of cold piss tearing up five-pound notes.

GALE: Oh God, I'm sorry.

ALKO: So I should hope! By the standards of a great many people, you know, we're poor, and you just throw your money around — the trouble is that you're just like everybody else in England — the class system has made you afraid of affluence without responsibility. But if bringing up a family's not a responsible business, I don't know what is.

GALE: It's my money!

(Pause.)

Well, most of it.

ALKO: Christ! You act irrationally when you're threatened with a crisis, and when you're not threatened you don't act at all!

GALE: I don't want to lose Joan!

(MARIEN and ROBERT are both laughing naturally at this.)

ALKO: Be realistic; we are in competition with the working classes for the means of support — I'm going to make sure I have them, and that goes for my family as well. Joan is not the family, she is the servant, and if she doesn't like it she can get out and work somewhere else!

(JOAN starts pouring the whisky into paper cups and handing it round.)

MARIEN: My God is that whisky. I'll probably get drunk on just the smell.

JOAN: Actually, it's not whisky, it's my wages.

ROBERT: We haven't had a drink since we moved here. If you give up alcohol, you start having different dreams.

ALKO: Marien, are you going to move out of here when you have your child.

MARIEN: I don't know . . . I stopped taking the pill six months ago. We've had arguments, about planning a family. Robert doesn't think one should plan.

ROBERT: I've had a sperm test. It's not my end of the apparatus at all. It is Marien's acidic womb. In addition to being past safe childbearing age she has difficulty creating a friendly climate for them. When I was in hospital I used to have fantasies about Marien's huge clitoris, the size of a blacksmith's apron, scooping out the semen and firing them in a dense hail past her knees. Rather like a Roman catapult and a handful of dried beans. Now alas all the action takes place on a molecular level, and so my appreciation becomes correspondingly microscopic.

(Pause.)

I don't mean it's like a retort where the little things go up in clouds of green smoke. Their life I imagine as a sort of marshy expedition when finally, through lack of forage in the alien country, they perish.

(He drinks.)

ALKO: How disappointing for you.

ROBERT: It's probably all for the best. Mother Nature is beavering away somewhere in the swamp. Who knows, come the spring, the geography of the uterus may suddenly improve.

(Pause.)

MARIEN (in protest): I was so looking forward to seeing you – Robert –

ALKO (trying to steer the conversation back): Do you regret giving your money away, Robert?

ROBERT (offhand): The rain comes through the roof.

ALKO: Isn't that hard?

ROBERT: You had an argument with your wife and employee just now. Your face went red, you trembled where you stood. You appeared to be dying of apoplexy guarding what you think is yours. You wish it to be yours in order to be secure in your longevity. Whatever you do is hard. But I'd rather be my hard than your hard.

ALKO: This is a semi-industrial country Robert! We can't all live like fucking gippos!

ROBERT: Your greed is astounding.

ALKO: I have security.

ROBERT: The sabbath goat. Is sitting out there in the field, its yellow goaty eyes fixed on the world about it. In its tiny mind, there have as yet been no signs from the universe fixing its doom. It is dreaming of fields of print. Go and meet it. It is proud like you. We are going to eat it for supper.

MARIEN: Gale's seen it.

ROBERT: Take the other two darling and show them the goat.

ALKO (exciting): A goat, eh.

JOAN: There's nothing special about goats. We used to have goats.

MARIEN: No! It's terribly exciting!

ALKO: Goats, huh.

(MARIEN, ALKO and JOAN go out and the flap closes, leaving ROBERT and GALE alone on the stage.)

GALE: In many ways he's an ideal husband, solid, dependable, reliable . . . I know it's not entirely what I wanted, but it's what a bit of me wanted . . .

(ROBERT is peering into the pram.)

And, Robert, I don't need to be stoked, I'm not frigid any more, we both exude sexual competence.

(ROBERT makes faces at the child in the pram. Puts his fingers in his mouth and pulls it open.)

ROBERT: And is this all you've got to show for all that talk?

GALE: I'm really not very good with infants – I couldn't have managed without Joan.

ROBERT: So your life is now indifferent motherhood via a cheap labour pool. What a rotten world for the baby Jesus to come into.

GALE: He's sweet when he's asleep, but I don't think he's going to be Jesus.

ROBERT: You didn't use to withdraw, Gale, you used to be social, quite lively. Not just repressed sexuality either. You had a lovely mind. Where did you put it? I can't but suspect that the foundation of your relationship with your husband is cracked and you find yourself out of place. I'm right aren't I.

GALE: Yes, but no prizes.

ROBERT: I can't believe that great bore flattens you that much.

GALE: We're all getting timid and lazy.

(ROBERT peers outside the tent craftily

Suddenly ROBERT starts to undress GALE. She makes no resistance, nor does she help him.)

GALE: Childbearing is meant to alter your metabolism but it hasn't done anything to mine.

ROBERT: Gypsies have their children in ditches.

GALE: I was never good at getting out of situations — it's insecurity. I don't want to move. I thought Marien was the insecure one.

ROBERT: She's got love. Hurry up, they'll be back in a minute.

GALE: Is adultery *different*?

ROBERT: What happens here doesn't matter a damn except for happinesss. Hardly likely to jeopardise eternal life here are we. Come on.

GALE: Ow —

(They get on the swan in a flurry of discarding clothes.

They disappear mostly behind the wings.)

ROBERT: No time for mucking about. Come on Gale, why aren't you doing something with your life?

GALE: Somewhere — in my upbringing — right at the bottom — I thought — that it would be — enough —

ROBERT: It's not! — Everybody's got to know what they are doing —

GALE: You're ruining my tights.

ROBERT: You're a lazy bitch. You're doing nothing.

GALE: It takes a lot of time having a child.

(The lights are changing. They become a low golden pool in the centre.)

ROBERT: So what. God's energies are in my arms and my shoulders and my cock right now, I see him in the clouds and if it isn't the same for you you've only yourself to blame. I'm not revitalising you. You've got to do it for yourself.

GALE: Oh.

ROBERT: People change! They can change! They do change!

GALE: They just suffer more or less.

ROBERT: No!

GALE: Really Robert, this is ridiculous. I don't know what we're doing!

(The humming-top noise, recorded, fades in very quickly.)

ROBERT: We're moving!

(The static comes in underneath.)

GALE: From where to where?

(A row of coloured bulbs in the circus furniture starts to flash.)

ROBERT: We're helping to turn the earth.

GALE: Oh.

ROBERT: Well don't ignore it!

(Blackout.

Cut the sound cues suddenly. A sudden, long, shout from GALE as she comes. A single steady red bulb in the row comes on.)

GALE'S VOICE-OVER TAPED: Gale's novel, the novel with a key. I went outside. It was the only time I saw flying saucers. It was the last time I saw Robert, the discoverer of miracles, demons and innocence . . . I never told Alko. He had an affair with Joan, who left. He never told me. We weren't particularly happy, we didn't do very much and we weren't honest with each other. I wrote a book about religious ecstasy. It was said I did not understand it.

(The red light dies.

Lights. ROBERT is sitting glumly in the middle of the tent arms out-stretched. MARIEN is sitting watching him.)

ROBERT: I've got rheumatism.

(Pause.)

So put a bucket under the rip, Marien, it'll rain.

MARIEN: Don't boss me about!

(She moves the bucket.)

They said we could go and stay any time. Gale's looking terribly well I thought . . . Joan's a sweet girl too.

(MARIEN gets a ledger out.)

ROBERT: There's no point in jeopardising one's view of eternity by spending a weekend in Sittingbourne. It'd turn into a week, a month, two months. They'll be afraid to let us go, afraid to turn us out. The whole thing would be a burden on everyone.

(Dictates smoothly to MARIEN.)

Today. Today I saw, 10 a.m. three flying saucers towards Whitby. Luminous cones. They did not signal. 11 a.m. the magical tree spoke to me. It feared the future of mankind. I stroked its branches. 3 p.m. primal force with a message. I think it was 'eel'. 6 p.m., I entered Gale.

MARIEN (throws down the book, glares at him): That's a poor excuse for adultery!

Me! What about me! I just seem to be some sort of doormat in your games! I've stayed with you, I've lived with you, I've seen your madness through to this bitter end, and I still love you. I love you enough to want to have a child by you. You and not Alko or anyone else. I want to go where we can have a child. And we can't do it here. My body knows that. That's why I can't conceive here! The winter's coming Robert! It's November! I want love, security with you, and warmth!

ROBERT (quietly mock-reasonable): I've explained to you time and again Marien that we're trying to do without the state of mind that plans for the future. It's not the future that matters. God provides the future. And every time I say that to you, you say yes I see and five minutes later you come back with a pathetic request for some toilet object.

MARIEN: Robert I have given you the better part of my life. What the rest of it's going to be like I just can't imagine. We haven't conquered material objects here. They've won. When you were rich we were free to do anything. All right we made a mess of it. But for the love of God give us freedom to choose.

ROBERT: I am sorry that your love was not given freely. If it's a habit you should break it. We're not married in this country. We don't own each other. We don't own anything. Not a stick, not a child, nothing. We are free.

MARIEN: But I saved you! You owe it to me!

ROBERT: You can't owe anyone love. Anything owed is guilt. If you put yourself in a position where you think you're owed something and you're not, it's just too bad. Freedom is the only thing which matters. Now get the supper.

MARIEN: Don't boss me about!

(She goes out.

She half leans back into the tent.)

VOICE: Mr Robert Martin.

MARIEN: Er . . . yes . . . he's in there . . .

(A figure comes in wearing a coat, with a trilby and moustache. It is MACK. He has inherited ROBERT's mantle of materialism. He is odious, patronising and triumphant.

MARIEN still in a huff leaves. MACK takes off his hat, smiles at ROBERT.)

ROBERT: Who?

MACK: Mack.

ROBERT: I don't employ servants any more.

MACK: I'm not a servant. I've come to serve a writ on you.

ROBERT: D'you mean you're a bloody bum bailiff. In Pickering. Dear God, you're illiterate. How did you get here, and get the Council to employ you.

(MACK tapes a polythene-wrapped notice to one of the tent poles.)

MACK: I'm not illiterate.

ROBERT: You're an imposter.

MACK (points to notice): Whereas. That's how it starts. Whereas. Whereas twenty-four hours' notice to clear out. Trespass, sanitary risk to the council estate . . .

(Pause.)

And the rest is threats about alsatians.

ROBERT: Things have come to a pretty pass when the lower classes knife and boot their way into the private armies of bureaucracy.

MACK: Whereas.

ROBERT: You odious little punk.

MACK: You can't say that to me. Not any more. See, you don't own anything. Don't own any property. I've got a wife, two kids and we bought a council house. Whereas —

(Finger on nose.)

See yer tomorrow. Whereas.

(Goes out. Pause. A dreadful crash.

MARIEN comes back in leading a small goat.

She starts stropping a cutthroat razor.)

ROBERT: That was Mack.

MARIEN: I didn't recognise him.

ROBERT: He's the Pickering bailiff. He's chucking us out.

MARIEN: Who'll look after the circus then?

ROBERT: They'll take it away and burn it.

MARIEN: Was he pleased to see you?

ROBERT: You know, I think he still can't read.

MARIEN: You know I was saying we had come to the end — well in a sense it's true, and I'm quite glad we're leaving, but I'm sorry really that they're going to make a bonfire of all this.

ROBERT: We've no money. We've nowhere to go.

MARIEN: You're planning!

ROBERT: Only negatively. I don't regret giving away my money, in fact it was the only thing that preserved my grasp on the world, but from time to time I do regret, intensely, the demeaning effects of poverty.

MARIEN (moving to the goat): Can you hold its neck and I'll draw.

(They hold the goat down. MARIEN prepares to slit its throat.

The rain starts.)

MARIEN: I've put the bucket in the wrong place Robert. I'll move it.

ROBERT: Let it come down.

MARIEN: We're not going to go on the road again are we?

ROBERT: With a bit of luck there'll be a millenium this year.

MARIEN: Did you foresee one?

ROBERT: What makes me so furious is that every tinpot mystic for the last three thousand years has seen one — and there's been nothing. It's a worthless trade.

(ROBERT for the first time we see utterly depressed.)

MARIEN: Perhaps you could try something else.

ROBERT: It's this or the madhouse. This time it'll be for good. There's nothing in front of us, except old age, sickness and death. Oh, why was I born.

(Brief tableau. Suddenly, as if from a great distance, 'Non, Je Ne Regrette Rien', solo vocal.

AEROPLANE PARKER, a wet, jolly Frenchman with a beret, striped shirt, Maizepaper Boyar out of his mouth, soggy bread under his arm, makes a sudden entrance through the tent flaps at the back.)

PARKER: Bonsoir, les Anglais! Fucken wet eh. Wet fucken. Cor. Cunt. Wet. Ello. Ça marche, Robert? Mon petit voyou, pourquoi tu ne restes pas dans la ville en cette merde de temps?

(He dances about gaily.)

J'ai dit, Why do — you — stay — 'ere, you mad bugger.

(Sees goat.)

Bon dieu de putain, qu'est que tu fais ici. Crotte de chevre?! Ze little goat has shat wiz surprise at seeing how I am wet.

(Throws the little goat out of doors.)

Soon ze little goat too will be wet. Va-t'en.

(He kisses ROBERT and MARIEN.

The distant singing is coming closer.)

We have come back. We have returned. We have permits for performing. America, Rome, Paris, Spain. You can be clown in Los Angeles.

(Another typical Frenchman enters and starts rounding up the props etc., dancing with MARIEN.)

MARIEN: They're coming tomorrow to tear it down —

PARKER: Jus let zem try it wiz Airplane Parker. Wiz twenty of ze boys from Lyons —

(The rest of the cast, dressed as Frenchman arrive.

The record of 'Je Ne Regrette Rien' takes over.

Bonsoir, Zob-nez!

ZOBNEZ: Bonsoir, tout le monde!!

(All embrace. The music continues.)

PARKER: Tomorrow it is sunny. You will come wiz us. Around the world. Hotels, brothels, railway arches. Let me feel your smashing bum Marien.

(Embraces MARIEN.)

'E fucks around so you do ze same darlink. Of course you must come. 'E is so serious about his life. We are so little. Like zer little goats. We must explore zer world. Moi, j'ai choisi l'existentialisme — stop writing your stupid book. Get pissed and do a little dance. 'E can be ze clown, and you can be zer lady on zer swan. God wants to see you on zer tight-rope and zer crowd staring up your knickers. Anyzing else he want you to do, he is a dumb bugger.

(The music swells. Funny noses are given out.)

PARKER: Very good. Yes everybody dance now. Fucking dance.

(They dance off, then dance back to 'At the Hop'.

The audience put on the funny noses which have been provided in the programme and go out into the night.)

The end

METHUEN PLAYSCRIPTS

Michael Abbensetts	SWEET TALK
Paul Ableman	TESTS
	BLUE COMEDY
Andrei Amalrik	EAST-WEST and IS UNCLE JACK A CONFORMIST?
Ed Berman/Justin Wintle	THE FUN ART BUS
Barry Bermange	NATHAN AND TABILETH AND OLDENBERG
John Bowen	THE CORSICAN BROTHERS
Howard Brenton	REVENGE
	CHRISTIE IN LOVE and OTHER PLAYS
	PLAYS FOR PUBLIC PLACES
	MAGNIFICENCE
Henry Chapman	YOU WON'T ALWAYS BE ON TOP
Peter Cheeseman (Ed)	THE KNOTTY
Caryl Churchill	OWNERS
David Cregan	THREE MEN FOR COLVERTON
	TRANSCENDING AND THE DANCERS
	THE HOUSES BY THE GREEN
	MINIATURES
	THE LAND OF PALMS AND OTHER PLAYS
Alan Cullen	THE STIRRINGS IN SHEFFIELD ON SATURDAY NIGHT
Rosalyn Drexler	THE INVESTIGATION and HOT BUTTERED ROLL
Simon Gray	THE IDIOT
Henry Livings	GOOD GRIEF!
	THE LITTLE MRS FOSTER SHOW
	HONOUR AND OFFER
	PONGO PLAYS 1-6
	THIS JOCKEY DRIVES LATE NIGHTS
	THE FFINEST FFAMILY IN THE LAND
	EH?
John McGrath	EVENTS WHILE GUARDING THE BOFORS GUN
David Mercer	THE GOVERNOR'S LADY
Georges Michel	THE SUNDAY WALK
Rodney Milgate	A REFINED LOOK AT EXISTENCE
Guillaume Oyono-Mbia	THREE SUITORS: ONE HUSBAND and UNTIL FURTHER NOTICE
Alan Plater	CLOSE THE COALHOUSE DOOR
David Selbourne	THE PLAY OF WILLIAM COOPER AND EDMUND DEW-NEVETT
	THE TWO-BACKED BEAST
	DORABELLA

Wole Soyinka	CAMWOOD ON THE LEAVES
Johnny Speight	IF THERE WEREN'T ANY BLACKS
	YOU'D HAVE TO INVENT THEM
Martin Sperr	TALES FROM LANDSHUT
Boris Vian	THE KNACKER'S ABC
Lanford Wilson	HOME FREE! and THE MADNESS
	OF LADY BRIGHT
Harrison, Melfi, Howard	NEW SHORT PLAYS
Duffy, Harrison, Owens	NEW SHORT PLAYS: 2
Barker, Grillo, Haworth,	NEW SHORT PLAYS: 3
Simmons	

METHUEN'S MODERN PLAYS

Edited by John Cullen and Geoffrey Strachan

Paul Ableman	GREEN JULIA
Jean Anouilh	ANTIGONE
	BECKET
	POOR BITOS
	RING ROUND THE MOON
	THE LARK
	THE REHEARSAL
	THE FIGHTING COCK
	DEAR ANTOINE
	THE DIRECTOR OF THE OPERA
John Arden	SERJEANT MUSGRAVE'S DANCE
	THE WORKHOUSE DONKEY
	ARMSTRONG'S LAST GOODNIGHT
	LEFT-HANDED LIBERTY
	SOLDIER, SOLDIER AND OTHER PLAYS
	TWO AUTOBIOGRAPHICAL PLAYS
John Arden and	THE BUSINESS OF GOOD GOVERNMENT
Margaretta D'Arcy	THE ROYAL PARDON
	THE HERO RISES UP
Ayckbourn, Bowen,	MIXED DOUBLES
Brook, Campton, Melly,	
Owen, Pinter, Saunders,	
Weldon	
Brendan Behan	THE QUARE FELLOW
	THE HOSTAGE
	RICHARD'S CORK LEG
Barry Bermange	NO QUARTER AND THE INTERVIEW
Edward Bond	SAVED
	NARROW ROAD TO THE DEEP NORTH
	THE POPE'S WEDDING

Harold Pinter	THE BIRTHDAY PARTY
	THE ROOM and THE DUMB WAITER
	THE CARETAKER
	A SLIGHT ACHE AND OTHER PLAYS
	THE COLLECTION and THE LOVER
	THE HOMECOMING
	TEA PARTY AND OTHER PLAYS
	LANDSCAPE AND SILENCE
	OLD TIMES
David Selbourne	THE DAMNED
Jean-Paul Sartre	CRIME PASSIONNEL
Wole Soyinka	MADMEN AND SPECIALISTS
	THE JERO PLAYS
Boris Vian	THE EMPIRE BUILDERS
Peter Weiss	TROTSKY IN EXILE
Theatre Workshop	OH WHAT A LOVELY WAR
and Charles Chilton	
Charles Wood	'H'
	VETERANS
Carl Zuckmayer	THE CAPTAIN OF KOPENICK

METHUEN'S THEATRE CLASSICS

THE TROJAN WOMEN	Euripides
	an English version by Neil Curry
THE BACCHAE OF EURIPIDES	an English version by Wole Soyinka
THE REDEMPTION	Moliere
	translated by Richard Wilbur
LADY PRECIOUS STREAM	adapted by S. I. Hsiung from a sequence of traditional Chinese plays
IRONHAND	Goethe
	adapted by John Arden
THE GOVERNMENT INSPECTOR	Gogol
	an English version by Edward O. Marsh and Jeremy Brooks
DANTON'S DEATH	Buechner
	an English version by James Maxwell
LONDON ASSURANCE	Boucicault
	adapted and edited by Ronald Eyre
BRAND	Ibsen
HEDDA GABLER	translated by Michael Meyer
THE WILD DUCK	
THE MASTER BUILDER	
GHOSTS	

If you would like regular information
on new Methuen plays, please write to
The Marketing Department
Eyre Methuen Ltd
North Way
Andover
Hants

(Pause. The actors begin to disperse. Then, sudden fade as they move.
Sound cue, Jagger, 'Memo from Mr Turner'. Followed by Grace Slick
singing 'Chauffeur'.)

ACT TWO

The audience, summoned from the bar by the GORILLAS, start to sit down again. With the house lights still on, the GORILLAS come forward to address them.

GORILLA 1: All life is a tension between sex and death. Men long for one or the other all the time. They are the ultimate yearnings. Because, most of the time, neither of these ultimate urges is being achieved, men find it necessary to build civilisations to try and cover over these basic urges.

(And now they both start talking separately to different parts of the audience at the same time.)

GORILLA 1: The pleasure principle. What we really want at the bottom of it all is to have a good time, a really good time.

But it isn't easy to have a good time nowadays. You can't make love to everybody, all the time, so there are bound to be disappointments in life . . . But you can have a good time some of the time . . . If you don't go too far.

I hope you're enjoying yourselves. I hope you're getting pleasure. That's *our* pleasure principle. You know it makes sense. Stay with us. Don't make mistakes. Quietly to the grave.

GORILLA 2: At the bottom of it all we want to have the best time of all, and in practical terms we always settle for less. We always frustrate those sudden urges. Tonight, the middle way, a little pleasure. Not too much of anything, because in this world you lose it all that way, you end up unhappy, or dead . . .

That's *our* pleasure principle. No extravagant responses, please, from you. Don't slash the seats. Don't piss in the stalls. It may be less rewarding, but you're in civilisation, you've got to sit back for the moment and enjoy the view. Have fun. Nobody's digging anybody's grave tonight. No lunatics in the audience tonight I hope. No . . . unbalanced persons . . . we don't want anybody to go too far. Don't try to fuck *everybody*. Don't kill yourself trying to take over the world.

(When GORILLA 1 has finished his speech, he starts speaking GORILLA 2's, and when 2 has finished his he goes on to 1's.

At the end, one GORILLA jumps into the other's arms and says as they go off.)

GORILLA 1: And now, to finish the interval, a cautionary tale about someone who went too far —

(They exit. The house lights stay on.)

VOICE: Ernst Hanfstangl was a contemporary of T. S. Eliot at Harvard, and was for many years close to Hitler.

HANFSTANGL VOICE (elderly, German-American accent): My wife said, Putzi, that fellow is a neuter. What he was doing when he made his speeches, was making love to the whole of Germany, because he was impotent the only outlet for this enormous nervous energy, was oratory.

And there is no doubt, he was a genius, within the narrow provincial vision that made him think of the world as one big sportpalatz. But his sexual energies were perverted and twisted because they could find no outlet. He took beautiful actresses out for the night: in the morning, they would give the thumbs-down.

(The house lights start to go down.)

When his earliest putsch at the Feldenhalle failed, he was in my house when the police came. I had fled to Austria. He took his revolver and said, this is the end, I will never let these swine take me. I will shoot myself first. And my wife — one of the few ju-jitsu holds I had taught here — I'll show you — give me your hand.

(The house lights are extinguished.

The set is window stage right, french window stage left.

The orange light behind comes up, suggestive of a sodium-lit street at night.

No more lighting for the moment.

As HANFSTANGL continues his story, a figure in a high peaked cap, long coat, is silhouetted crossing stage right to left, with the silhouette on the windows.

It pauses outside the french windows where it is in full silhouette, and raises the gun to its head, level with its temple.

The figure remains like that in tableau for the rest of the speech.)

HANFSTANGL (continuing without a break): — and she disarmed him. She threw the revolver into a bowl of flour we kept in the attic.

Hitler was in love like a mooncalf with my wife, and when they had put him in prison he wanted to follow the example of the Sinn Feiners and go on hunger-strike — my wife sent a message to him, she had not prevented him from committing suicide in order to let him starve to death. This advice from a beautiful woman turned the scale and he called it off.

When he was in jail, surrounded and his mind poisoned by his cronies, the worst sort of provincial anti-semites, I went to see him with my son. He had a marvellous way with children and Egon adored him. But there was never any sign of his private life having a sexual outlet that in everybody is essential and normal.

(The figure behind the french window suddenly drops the gun and darts out of sight.

The lights immediately come up at the end of HANFSTANGL's story to show the interior of GALE's London flat, which is a large first-floor room with french windows leading out on to a balcony.

Stage left an entrance to the kitchen through red, white and blue plastic drapes. Upstage left a double bed under the window. Next to it midstage, against the wall, is a table with a telephone and a stool or pouffe, stage left the french windows. Extreme stage left there is no exit apparent, the end of the room a jumble of unsuitable furniture, cheap thirties armchairs, contrasting strongly with the fitted drawers and louvred cupboard doors with the unmistakable look of a nasty yet professional conversion job.

The flat is the model for affluence gone sour. It has no particular style. There are dirty plates and cups everywhere, perched on every available extrusion.

The drawers are all throwing their contents out on the floor in the classic burgled pattern, the lower ones completely out, the top ones partially out.

One of the walls is mauve, another is red oxide.

There are sundry notices pinned on them, mostly in handwriting illegible to the audience. One visible notice is the front page of the *Daily Express* for 25 November 1972 which says MARTIN BORMANN ALIVE.

As the lights come up, GALE is asleep in the bed, as is MACK. JOAN is asleep on the balcony.

The door out of sight in the kitchen slams. GALE sits up in bed like a jack-in-a-box and looks round wildly.)

MARIEN's VOICE (from the kitchen): Oh! This is monstrous! How disgusting!

(GALE immediately leaps out of bed and puts on a crumpled long white flannel dressing-gown over pants, but no bra.

She swiftly collects three dirty saucers and mugs, then her initiative grinds to a halt and she stands in the middle of the room, momentarily nonplussed.

Pause.

MARIEN makes something of an entrance through the plastic strips, which are dealt with briskly. She is wearing a blue suit trimmed with white edging, and a blue closely-woven raffia hat.

Formidable. We see what she is carrying before her: it is a partially unwrapped, partially used half pound of butter on a plate.)

MARIEN: Ugh! This is rancid. I don't know how you can bear it — with this around, it's a wonder you can bring yourself to eat at all. Horrid.

Durkheim, E. 1966 [1897]. *Suicide*. New York: Free Press.

Eder, D. and L. Fingerson. 2002. 'Interviewing Children and Adolescents.' pp. 181–201 in *Handbook of Interview Research: Context and Method*, edited by J. Gubrium and J. Holstein. Thousand Oaks, CA: Sage.

Ellis, C. and A. Bochner. 1992. 'Telling and Performing Personal Stories: The Constraints of Choice in Abortion.' pp. 70–101 in *Investigating Subjectivity* edited by C. Ellis and M. G. Flaherty. Newbury Park, CA: Sage.

Ellis, C. and A. P. Bochner. 1996. 'Talking Over Ethnography.' pp. 13–45 in *Composing Ethnography: Alternative Forms of Qualitative Writing*, edited by C. Ellis and A. Bochner. Walnut Creek, CA: AltaMira Press.

Ellis, C. and A. P. Bochner. 2000. 'Autoethnography, Personal Narrative, Reflexivity: Researcher as Subject.' pp. 733–768 in *Handbook of Qualitative Research*, 2nd ed., edited by N. Denzin and Y. Lincoln. Thousand Oaks, CA: Sage.

Emerson, R. 1988. *Contemporary Field Research: A Collection of Readings*. Prospect Heights, IL, Waveland Press.

Evans, J. and S. Hall. 1999. *Visual Culture: The Reader*. London: Sage.

Filmer, P., M. Phillipson, D. Silverman and D. Walsh. 1973. *New Directions in Sociological Theory*. Cambridge, MA: MIT Press.

Flaherty, M., N. Denzin, P. Manning and D. Snow. 'Review Symposium: Crisis in Representation.' *Journal of Contemporary Ethnography* 31(4): 478–516.

Fleisher, M. S. 1995. *Beggars and Thieves: Lives of Urban Street Criminals*. Madison, WI: The University of Wisconsin Press.

Fontana, A. 2002. 'Postmodern Trends in Interviewing.' pp. 161–80 in *Handbook of Interview Research: Context and Method*, edited by J. Gubrium and J. Holstein. Thousand Oaks, CA: Sage.

Fontana, A. and J. Frey. 2000. 'The Interview: From Structured Questions to Negotiated Text.' pp. 645–672 in *Handbook of Qualitative Research*, 2nd ed., edited by N. Denzin and Y. Lincoln. Thousand Oaks, CA: Sage.

Foucault, M. 1977. *Discipline and Punish: The Birth of the Prison*. New York: Vintage.

Foucault, M. 1980. *Power/Knowledge*, edited by C. Gordon. New York: Pantheon Books.

Fowler, F. J. 1991. 'Reducing Interviewer-Related Error through Interviewer Training, Supervision, and Other Means.' pp. 269–278 in *Measurement Errors in Surveys*, edited by P. P. Biemer, R. M. Groves, L. E. Lyberg, N. A. Mathiowetz and S. Sudman. New York: John Wiley.

Frazier, C., D. Bishop, L. Lanza–Kaduce and A. Marvasti. 1999. 'Juveniles in Criminal Court: Past and Current Research from Florida.' *Quinnipiac Law Review*, 10: 573–596.

Garfinkel, H. 1967. *Studies in Ethnomethodology*. Englewood Cliffs, NJ: Prentice Hall.

Geertz, C. 1988. 'Thick Description: Toward an Interpretive Theory of Culture.' pp. 37–59 in *Contemporary Field Research: A Collection of Readings*, edited by R. Emerson. Prospect Heights, IL, Waveland Press.

General Social Survey. 1998. Chicago: National Opinion Research Center.

Gill, R. 2000. 'Discourse Analysis.' pp. 172–190 in *Qualitative Researching with Text, Image and Sound*. M. Bauer and G. Gaskell Eds. London: Sage.

Glaser, B. and A. Srauss. 1967. *The Discovery of Grounded Theory: Strategies for Qualitative Research*. Chicago, IL: Aldine.

Goffman, E. 1959. *The Presentation of Self in Everyday Life*. Garden City, NY: Anchor Books, Doubleday.

Goffman, E. 1979. *Gender Advertisements*. Cambridge, MA: Harvard University Press.

Goffman, E. 1981. *Forms of Talk*. Philadelphia: University of Pennsylvania Press.

Goffman, E. 1993. 'The Moral Career of the Mental Patient.' pp. 413–426 in *Social Deviance: Readings in Theory and Research*, edited by H. Pontell. Englewood Cliffs, NJ: Prentice Hall.

Gray, J. 1993. *Men, Women, and Relationships*. New York: Harper.

Grills, S. 1998a. 'An Invitation to the Field: Fieldwork and the Pragmatists' Lesson' pp. 3–20 in *Doing Ethnographic Research: Fieldwork Settings*, edited by S. Grills. Thousand Oaks, CA: Sage.

Grills, S. 1998b. 'On Being Partisan in Non-Partisan Settings: Field Research Among the Politically Committed.' pp. 76–93 in *Doing Ethnographic Research: Fieldwork Settings*, edited by S. Grills. Thousand Oaks, CA: Sage.

Gubrium, J. 1992. *Out of Control: Family Therapy and Domestic Disorder*. Newbury Park, CA: Sage.

Gubrium, J. 1993. *Speaking of Life: Horizons of Meaning for Nursing Home Residents*. Hawthorne, NY: Aldine de Gruyter.

Gubrium, J. and J. Holstein. 1997a. *The New Language of Qualitative Method*. New York: Oxford University Press.

Gubrium, J. and J. Holstein. 1997b. 'Narrative Practice and the Coherence of Personal Stories.' *The Sociological Quarterly* 39(1): 163–187.

Gubrium, J. F. and J. A. Holstein. 2001. *Institutional Selves: Troubled Identities in a Postmodern World*. New York, N.Y.: Oxford University Press.

Gubrium, J. and J. Holstein. 2002. 'From the Individual Interview to Interview Society.' pp. 3–32 in *Handbook of Interview Research: Context and Method*, edited by J. Gubrium and J. Holstein. Thousand Oaks, CA: Sage.

Hammersley, M. 1990. *Reading Ethnographic Research: A Critical Guide*. London: Longmans.

Hammersley, M. and P. Atkinson. 1983. *Ethnography: Principles in Practice*. London: Routledge.

Harper, D. 1994. 'On the Authority of the Image: Visual Methods at the Crossroads.' pp. 403–412 in *Handbook of Qualitative Research*, edited by N. Denzin and Y. Lincoln. Thousand Oaks, CA: Sage.

Harper, D. 2000. 'Re-imagining Visual Methods: Galileo to Neuromancer.' pp. 717–732 in *Handbook of Qualitative Research*, 2nd ed., edited by N.K. Denzin and Y. Lincoln. Thousand Oaks, CA: Sage.

Heath, C. 1989. 'Pain Talk: The Expression of Suffering in the Medical Consulation.' *Social Psychology Quarterly* 52(2): 113–125.

Heath, C. 1997. 'Using Video: Analyzing Activities in Face to Face Interaction.' pp. 183–200 in *Qualitative Research: Theory, Method and Practice*. London: Sage.

Heritage, J. 1997. 'Conversation Analysis and Institutional Talk.' pp. 161–182, *Qualitative Research: Theory, Method and Practice*, edited by D. Silverman. London: Sage.

Heyl, B. S. 1977. 'The Madam as Teacher: The Training of House Prostitutes.' *Social Problems* 24: 545–555.

Heyl, B. S. 2001. 'Ethnographic Interviewing.' pp. 369–383 in *Handbook of Ethnography*, edited by P. Atkinson, A. Coffey, S. Delamont, J. Lofland and L. Lofland. London: Sage.

Hirschi, T. and M. Gottfredson (Eds.). 1994. *The Generality of Deviance*. New Brunswick, N.J.: Transaction.

Hodge, R. and G. Kress. 1988. *Social Semiotics*. Ithaca, NY: Cornell University Press.

Holstein, J. 1992. 'Producing People: Descriptive Practice in Human Service Work.' pp. 23–39 in *Perspectives on Social Problems*, vol. 6, edited by G. Miller and J. Holstein.

Holstein, J. and J. Gubrium. 1995. *The Active Interview*. Thousand Oaks, CA: Sage.

Holstein, J. and J. Gubrium. 1997. 'Active Interviewing.' pp. 113–129 in *Qualitative Research: Theory, Method, and Practice*, edited by David Silverman. London: Sage.

Holstein, J. and J. Gubrium. 2000. *The Self We Live By: Narrative Identity in a Postmodern World*. New York: Oxford University Press.

Huberman, M. and M. Miles. 1994. 'Data Management and Analysis Methods.' pp. 428–444 in *Handbook of Qualitative Research*, edited by N. Denzin and Y. Lincoln. Thousand Oaks, CA: Sage.

Humphreys, L. 1970. *Tearoom Trade: Impersonal Sex in Public Places*. Chicago: Aldine.

Janis, I. 1972. *Victims of Groupthink*. Boston: Houghton Mifflin.

Johnson, J. M. 2002. 'In-depth Interviewing.' pp. 103–119 in *Handbook of Interview Research: Context and Method*, edited by J. Gubrium and J. Holstein. Thousand Oaks, CA: Sage.

Jones, J. H. 1981. *Bad Blood*. New York: Free Press.

Kong, T. S. K., D. Mahoney and K. Plummer. 2002. 'Queering the Interview.' pp. 239–258 in *Handbook of Interview Research: Context and Method*, edited by J. Gubrium and J. Holstein. Thousand Oaks, CA: Sage.

Kuehnast, K. 1990. 'Gender Representation in Visual Ethnographies: An Interpretivist Perspective.' *Commission on Visual Anthropology Review* Spring: 21–29.

Lawton, J. 2002. 'Gaining and Maintaining Consent: Ethical Concerns Raised in a Study of Dying Patients.' *Qualitative Health Research* 11(5): 693–705.

Lincoln, Y. and E.G. Guba. 2000. 'Paradigmatic Controversies, Contradictions, and Emerging Confluences.' pp. 163–188 in *Handbook of Qualitative Research*, 2nd ed., edited by N. Denzin and Y. Lincoln. Thousand Oaks, CA: Sage.

Lofland, L. H. 1975. 'The Hereness of Women: A Selective Review of Urban Sociology.' pp. 144–170 in *Another Voice: Feminists Perspectives on Social Life and Social Science*, edited by M. M. Millan and R. M. Kanter. Garden City, NY: Anchor/Doubleday.

Lofland, J. and L. Lofland. 1995. *Analyzing Social Settings*. Belmont, CA: Wadsworth.

Loseke, D. and K. Fawcett. 1995. 'Appealing Appeals: Constructing Moral Worthiness, 1912–1927' *The Sociological Quarterly* 36: 61–77.

Lutz, C. A. and J. Collins. 1993. *Reading the National Geographic*. Chicago: The University of Chicago Press.

Macdonald, S. 2001. 'British Social Anthropology.' pp. 60–79 in *Handbook of Ethnography*, edited by P. Atkinson, A. Coffey, S. Delamont, J. Lofland and L. Lofland. London: Sage.

Macionis, J. 2001. *Sociology*, 8th ed. New Jersey: Prentice Hall.

Mahoney, D. 2000. Unpublished field notes for PhD. thesis. Department of Sociology, University of Essex.

Malinowski, B. 1929. *The Sexual Life of Savages in North-Western Melanesia*. New York: Halcyon House.

Mann, C. and F. Stewart. 2002. 'Internet Interviewing.' pp. 603–628 in *Handbook of Interview Research: Context and Method*, edited by J. R. Gubrium and J. Holstein. Thousand Oaks, CA: Sage.

Marvasti, A. 1998. '"Homelessness' as Narrative Redemption." pp. 167–182 in *Perspective on Social Problems*, vol 10, edited by G. Miller and J. Holstein. Greenwich, CT: JAI Press.

Marvasti, A. 2002. 'Constructing the Service-Worthy Homeless Through Narrative Editing.' *Journal of Contemporary Ethnography* 31(5): 615–651.

Marvasti, A. 2003. *Being Homeless: Textual and Narrative Constructions*. Langham, MD: Lexington Books.

Marvasti, A. and C. Faircloth. 2002. 'Writing the Exotic, the Authentic, and the Moral: Romanticism as Discursive Resource for the Ethnographic Text.' *Qualitative Inquiry* 8(6): 760–784.

Marvasti, A. and McKinney, K.D. Forthcoming. *Unwelcome Immigrants: Middle Eastern Lives in the U.S.* Langham, MD: Rowman and Littlefield.

Merton, R. K. 1938. 'Social Structure and Anomie.' *American Sociological Review* 3: 672–682.

Merton, R. K., M. Fiske and P. L. Kendall. 1956. *The Focused Interview*. Glencoe, IL: Free Press.

Messner, M., M. C. Duncan and K. Jensen. 1993. 'Separating the Men from the Girls: The Gendered Language of Televised Sports.' *Gender and Society* 7: 121–137.

Miller, G. and J. Holstein. 1995. 'Dispute Domains: Organizational Contexts and Dispute Processing.' *The Sociological Quarterly* 36(1): 37–59.

Morgan, D.L. 2002. 'Focus Group Interviewing.' pp. 141–160 in *Handbook of Interview Research: Context and Method*, edited by J. Gubrium and J. Holstein. Thousand Oaks, CA. Sage.

Perärkylä, A. 1997. 'Reliability and Validity in Research Based on Tapes and Transcripts.' pp. 201–220 in *Qualitative Research: Theory, Method and Practice*. London: Sage.

Pines, A. M. and M. H. Silbert. 1983. 'Early Sexual Exploitation as an Influence in Prostitution.' *Social Work* 28: 285–289.

Platt, J. 2002. 'The History of the Interview.' pp. 33–54 in *Handbook of Interview Research: Context and Method*, edited by J. Gubrium and J. Holstein. Thousand Oaks, CA: Sage.

Popper, K. 1959. *The Logic of Scientific Discovery*. New York: Basic.

Potter, K. 1996. 'Discourse Analysis and Constructionist Approaches: Theoretical Background.' pp. 125–140 in *Handbook of Qualitative Research Methods for Psychology and Social Sciences*, edited by J. Richardson. Leicester, England: BPS. Princeton University Press.

Prior, L. 1997. 'Following in Foucault's Footsteps.' pp. 63–79 in *Qualitative Research: Theory, Method and Practice*, edited by D. Silverman. London: Sage.

Quinn, B. A. 2002. 'Sexual Harassment and Masculinity: The Power and Meaning of "Girl Watching."' *Gender and Society* 16(3): 386–402.

Quinney, R. 1996. 'Once My Father Traveled West to California.' pp. 357–382 in *Composing Ethnography: Alternative Forms of Qualitative Writing*, edited by C. Ellis and A. Bochner. Walnut Creek, CA: AltaMira Press.

Reinhartz, S. and S. Chase. 2002. 'Interviewing Women.' pp. 221–238 in *Handbook of Interview Research: Context and Method*, edited by J. Gubrium and J. Holstein. Thousand Oaks, CA: Sage.

Remennick, L. I. and A. Hetsroni. 2001. 'Public Attitude toward Abortion in Israel: A Research Note.' *Social Science Quarterly* 82(2): 420–431.

Richardson, L. 1990a. 'Narrative and Sociology.' *Journal of Contemporary Ethnography* 19: 116–135.

Richardson, L. 1990b. *Writing Strategies: Researching Diverse Audiences*. Thousand Oaks, CA: Sage.

Riessman, C. K. 1990. *Divorce Talk: Women and Men Make Sense of Personal Relationships*. New Brunswick, NJ: Rutgers University Press.

Riessman, C. K. 1993. *Narrative Analysis*. Newbury Park, CA: Sage.

Riessman, K. R. 2002. 'Analysis of Personal Narratives.' pp. 695–710 in *Handbook of Interview Research: Context and Method*, J. Gubrium and edited by J. Holstein. Thousand Oaks, CA: Sage.

Ritzer, G. 2000. *Sociological Theory*. 5th ed. New York: McGraw-Hill.

Ronai, C. R. 1996. 'My Mother is Mentally Retarded.' pp. 109–131 in *Composing Ethnography: Alternative Forms of Qualitative Writing*, edited by C. Ellis and A. Bochner. Walnut Creek, CA: AltaMira Press.

Rose, G. 2001. *Visual Methodologies*. London: Sage.

Rosenau, P. M. 1992. *Postmodernism and the Social Sciences: Insights, Inroads, and Intrusions*. Princeton, NJ: Princeton University Press.

Rosenblatt, J. A. and M. J. Furlong. 1997. 'Assessing the Reliability and Validity of Student Self-Reports of Campus Violence.' *Journal of Youth and Adolescence* 26(2): 187–202.

Rubin, H. J. and I. S. Rubin. 1995. *Qualitative Interviewing: The Art of Hearing Data*. Thousand Oaks, CA: Sage.

Schaeffer, N. C. and D. W. Maynard. 2002. 'Standardization and Interaction in Survey Interviewing.' pp. 577–601 in *Handbook of Interview Research: Context and Method*, edited by J. Gubrium and J. Holstein. Thousand Oaks, CA: Sage.

Schmidtke, A., B. Weinacker, A. Apter and A. Batt. 1999. 'Suicide Rates in the World: Update,' *Archives of Suicide Research* 5: 81–89.

Schutz, A. 1967. *The Phenomenology of the Social World*. Evanston, IL: Northwestern University Press.

Schutz, A. 1971. 'The Stranger: An Essay in Social Psychology,' pp. 99–117 in *Alfred Schutz: Collected Paper II: The Problem of Social Reality*, edited by A. Broderson. The Hague: Martinus Nijohoff.

Schwandt, T. A. 2000. 'Three Epistemological Stances for Qualitative Inquiry: Interpretivism, Hermeneutics, and Social Constructionism.' pp. 189–213 in *Handbook of Qualitative Research*, 2nd ed., edited by N. Denzin and Y. Lincoln. Thousand Oaks, CA: Sage.

Schwalbe, M. L. and M. Wolkmoir. 2002. 'Interviewing Men.' pp. 203–219 in *Handbook of Interview Research: Context and Method*, edited by J. Gubrium and J. Holstein. Thousand Oaks, CA: Sage.

Seale, C. 2000. 'Using Computers to Analyse Qualitative Data.' pp. 154–175 in *Doing Qualitative Research: A Practical Handbook*, by D. Silverman. London: Sage.

Shaffir, W. 1998. 'Doing Ethnographic Research in Jewish Orthodox Communities: The Neglected Role of Stability.' pp. 48–64 in *Doing Ethnographic Research: Fieldwork Settings*, edited by S. Grills. Thousand Oaks, CA: Sage.

Silverman, D. 1985. *Qualitative Methodology and Sociology*. England: Gower.

Silverman, D. 1993. *Interpreting Qualitative Data: Methods for Analyzing Talk, Text, and Interaction*. London: Sage.

Silverman, D. 1997. *Qualitative Research: Theory, Method and Practice*. London: Sage.

Silverman, D. 2000. *Doing Qualitative Research: A Practical Handbook*. London: Sage.

Silverman, D. 2001. *Interpreting Qualitative Data: Method for Analyzing Talk, Text and Interaction*. 2nd ed, London: Sage.

Singleton, R. A. and B. Straits. 2002. 'Survey Interviewing.' pp. 59–82 in *Handbook of Interview Research: Context and Method*, edited by J. Gubrium and J. Holstein. Thousand Oaks, CA: Sage.

Small, S. A. 1995. 'Action-Oriented Research: Models and Methods.' *Journal of Marriage and Family* 57(4): 941–955.

Smith, D. E. 1996. 'The Relations of Ruling: A Feminist Inquiry.' *Studies in Culture Organizations and Societies* 2: 171–190.

Spencer, J. W. 2001. 'Self-Presentation and Organizational Processing in a Human Service Agency.' pp. 158-169 in *Institutional Selves: Troubled Identities in a Postmodern World*, edited by J. Gubrium and J. Holstein. New York, N.Y.: Oxford University Press.

Stasz, C. 1979. 'The Early History of Visual Sociology.' pp. 119–136 in *Images of Information: Still Photography in the Social Sciences*, edited by J. Wagner. Beverly Hills, CA: Sage.

Stein, G. 1980. 'Bilingual Battle: What Does It Mean?' *The Miami Herald*, August 3, p. 23A.

Strauss, A. and J. Corbin. 1990. *Basics of Qualitative Research: Grounded Theory Procedures and Techniques*. Newbury Park, CA: Sage.

Strauss, A. and J. Corbin. 1994. 'Grounded Theory Methodology: An overview.' pp. 273–285 in *Handbook of Qualitative Research*, edited by N. Denzin and Y. Lincoln. Thousand Oaks, CA: Sage.

Suchman, L. 1987. Plans and Situated Actions: *The Problem of Human-Machine Communication*. Cambridge: Cambridge University Press.

Taylor, J. M., C. Gilligan and A. M. Sullivan. 1995. *Between Voice and Silence: Women and Girls, Race and Relationship*. Cambridge, MA: Harvard University Press.

Tedlock, B. 2000. 'Ethnography and Ethnographic Representation.' pp. 455–486 in *Handbook of Qualitative Research*, 2nd ed., edited by N. Denzin and Y. Lincoln. Thousand Oaks, CA: Sage.

Valenzuela, A. 1999. *Subtractive Schooling: U.S.-Mexican Youth and the Politics of Caring*. Albany: State University of New York Press.

Van Ausdale, D. and J. Feagin. 2002. *The First R: How Children Learn Race and Racism*. Langham, MD: Rowman and Littlefield.

Van Maanen, J. 1988. *Tales from the Field*. Chicago: University of Chicago Press.

Vered, K. O. 1993. 'Feminist Ethnographic Films: Critical Viewing Required.' pp. 177–219 in *Anthropological Film and Video in the 1990s*, edited J. Rollwagon. Backport, NY: The Institute, Inc.

Vidich, A. J. and Stanford Lyman. 1985. *American Sociology: Worldly Rejections of Religion and Their Directions*. New Haven, MA: Yale University Press.

Warren, C. A. B. 1972. 'Observing the Gay Community'. in *Research on Deviance*, edited by J. D. Douglas. New York: Random House.

Weber, M. 1946. 'Science as a Vocation.' pp. 129–156 in *From Max Weber: Essays in Sociology*, edited and translated by Hans Gerth and C. Wright Mills. New York: Oxford University Press.

Weitzman, E. A. 2000. 'Software and Qualitative Research.' pp. 803–820 in *Handbook of Qualitative Research*. 2nd ed., edited by N. Denzin and Y. Lincoln. Thousand Oaks, CA: Sage.

Whyte, W. F. 1949. *Street Corner Society*. Chicago: University of Chicago Press.

Wolcott, Harry F. 2001. *Writing Up Qualitative Research*, 2nd ed. Thousand Oaks, CA: Sage.

World Health Organization. 1997. *Manual of the International Statistical Classification of Diseases, Injuries, and Causes of Death*, 9th ed. Geneva: WHO.

Index